Poison Into Medicine

My Life in a Doomsday Cult

Brandon W. Salo

ISBN: 978-1-7364024-0-5

Typeset in Garamond 11.5 by Brandon Walter Salo
Cover designed by Brandon Walter Salo

Author's Note

What follows is my life story. I've changed some names to protect the anonymity and safety of those who have suffered greatly at the hands of the House of Yahweh. Otherwise, every detail of this book is factual, in the best way I can remember it.

FAMILY BACKGROUND

I am the only child between my mother Romana, and my father Dale. I have one half-sister and one half-brother on my mother's side, and one half-sister on my father's side. I am also the youngest by at least 6 years. My childhood was separate from theirs, and as a result, a mystery to them... Until now.

PREFACE

Yisrayl has about 30 wives," Peter said as he approached, interrupting the group discussion. There were five of us standing in a circle in the dry Texas heat. All wearing worn work jeans, worn t-shirts and from rural white-American lower class. Some would simply write us off as white trash. Most people would never consider driving down the dirt roads to where we were having this conversation, if they knew it even existed, that is. Somehow us boys just ended up here. Our parents brought us. One thing that most of our parents had in common was that they all felt cheated in some way. Someone's wife left them, the government took something from them, they lost someone. In the end, I'm standing in a circle with other teenage boys who had just found society's backdoor to polygamy. What else was there to do, other than fantasize about how many wives we could have and how fun it would be to do whatever it was that we wanted to them? It's the type of talk you would assume from boys not too far past age of puberty, growing up in a polygamist cult.

"None of those marriages exist on paper, though. They all look like 'affairs' to the law out there." Peter pointed past the barbed-wire fence, off the compound. He pulled a bag of sunflower seeds from a pocket. "We don't need to acknowledge their laws for marriage. We don't break them, but it's Yahweh's law that matters." He tilted his head back and poured a handful of seeds into his mouth.

1

We were in rural bible-belt Texas. Anyone who doesn't know it, and those who only know it, have no idea that it's still the same wild west it was 150 years ago. Spaced apart one-hundred miles or so throughout the state is still some charismatic preacher, offering tickets to heaven and selling their own brand of snake oil. Some of them even sell in bulk. Some might only get heard about in a gun battle, like David Koresh in Waco. I had no idea where this cult would end up. I was just in it, and had been for about six years at this point.

We called them 'feasts', and this one had just ended. Everyone was preparing to leave. The compound grounds were dry, dusty and hot, as one might imagine the Bible-belt flatlands of Texas to be. On our way to and from there, we could drive for miles and miles down dirt roads with nothing to see but the stray longhorn. Tomorrow morning, we'd be heading back to the upper peninsula of Michigan. It was a 22-hour drive from Clyde, Texas, if we kept just above the speed limit and didn't stop to sleep.

I spent most of that ride home trying to wrap my head around having many wives, or my father having many wives, and me having more mothers. My father was a simple man; he said he didn't need more wives to keep things simple. My stepmother must have appreciated that sentiment. Although she knew she had no say in the matter, she was obviously content to be my father's only wife.

In another five months, we'd return to Texas. Three times a year we went, to pay our offerings and hear the latest teachings. We couldn't have guessed that the next new rule would be that the women had to wear burkas, and that a new barricade would be running through the sanctuary to separate the men from the women.

All of a sudden, men were not allowed to talk to any women unless they were married or directly related. If a man had a sister who was married, he couldn't talk to her unless he had specific permission from her husband. From now on, if I wanted to interact with any female, I would need to talk first with my father, then with the priests who oversaw our family. Those priests would then go to the girl's family's priests, and then talk with the girl's father. Assuming all this went well, I'd be permitted to speak to the girl.

"How is this going to work?" I wondered. I began to think that I'd be left out, and that only the older priests would be able to choose and marry who they wanted.

Up until that time, I'd simply had to ask an Elder for permission to talk to a girl. That's how I spoke to the first girl I was ever interested in. Her name was Karen. She was a very beautiful green-eyed blonde from California, new to the cult. I'd heard through the grapevine that she liked me. I had spoken to her a little before, but then I asked the Elder in contact with her parents whether I could 'start talking to her', meaning to pursue her for marriage. Elder Kepha took his time in the guise of teaching me patience before he approved. Eventually Karen and I were talking and flirting, as young teenagers do.

When the new rules came out (or "teachings", as the cult leaders liked to refer to them), I was told that Karen wasn't a virgin, and that if I ever wanted to become a priest,

I wouldn't be able to marry her. They said it would be best to stop pursuing her as a wife.

I didn't know what to think. Lost in a haze of puppy love, I thought I might be willing to give up a future in the priesthood. In any case it didn't matter; within a few months, her parents left the cult and went back to Fresno. I never saw her again.

About six months later, I remember making eye contact with another girl. I thought she was really pretty. I knew who she was because her father and mine were friends, and I looked up to him. He had a kind and gentle face and always made direct eye-contact with me when we spoke. He was a man who I respected naturally. Like my father he was hardworking and kind, which may be why I didn't think I was good enough to pursue his daughter in marriage, let alone ask for permission to speak to her.

Then a surprise: "She asked permission to speak to me?" I didn't even know it could work that way. My father told me it was unusual for a girl to pursue her husband in this manner, but since she had asked, I should accept the offer. Were I to enjoy her company, I could begin the process of betrothal. Certainly the formalities were peripheral – I couldn't help but be infatuated by her beauty.

I was 16 years old when this started. She must have been 14, going on 15. By that time, arranged marriages were becoming more and more common in the cult, and I thought to myself, "She could be the first of many young wives," as older men had often observed.

My spirits were elevated. My father could see that I had

more spring in my step. Every time we went to work in the forest, to cut down trees, I'd think about making money, building a house, and building my future family. I didn't know whether the cult prediction of the coming 'tribulation' would leave me time for all that. I didn't know whether I'd stay in high school or drop out. After all, the Elders told me that Armageddon would likely arrive before 2004.

In truth, I didn't know what to think, I just went along with it all. Looking back, I was simply unaware of a lot of things. Every week we'd have our religious ceremonies at home. We wouldn't leave the house, or do anything remotely like what we might in day-to-day life, such as watch television or shop or cook. Once a month, we'd drive six hours south to visit a group of cult members in Manitowoc, Wisconsin; then three times a year we'd drive all the way from Michigan to Texas, to the compound just outside Abilene. In the midst of all this, I was attending public schools, living two separate lives without the slightest clue. I was going with the flow, or else rolling with the punches, on every front.

"Repent or perish. If it's not forever, we don't want it," were a couple of their slogans. Yisrayl, the leader who would later crown himself 'King', was always telling us how close we were to the End, and how full of sin we all were. I guess because there was a girl who liked me, I ignored those extreme probabilities and allowed myself to get lost in my imagination.

I didn't exactly know what it would be like when I first spoke with her, but I did know it would all be very controlled and formal. I also knew that someone, an Elder, would approach me out of the blue and say "Now's the time you will meet her." Thankfully, I saw her father before I met her. Although the look in his eyes changed ever so slightly, he still sincerely approved.

When I first spoke to Samantha, it was in one of the office rooms of the cult sanctuary. We spoke through a gap between two cubicle partitions, with two priests and their wives on either side. They were positioned so that I couldn't see the women and Samantha couldn't see the men. They were taking notes of everything we said, to make sure there was nothing sinful happening. The conversations between us were almost pointless, since communication was done mainly with our eyes. I had seen her smile before, but whenever we spoke, she would wear a veil that covered her face.

We continued this unusual relationship until the summer of 2003. I was 17 and she was 15. We rarely spoke on the phone, and if we did, someone would be listening in. We mainly spoke on the compound during the cult gatherings that happened three times a year.

Then one Sunday morning, I woke up to a phone call at 8:00 a.m. It was the counselor who'd been monitoring my conversations with Samantha, along with everything else in my personal life that I'd ever confessed. He said bluntly, "Communication with Samantha is over with."

1. CHILDHOOD

My hands were soft, not callused; small and moist, fingers clenched to the floral-patterned comforter on my parent's bed. I was crying. Shouts between my mother and my father flew across the bedroom like bullets. I was in the crossfire, and I didn't know why.

My cries became louder and my mother grabbed me and said, "It's okay Brandon, it's okay."

I saw her look at my father with eyes suggesting it was all his fault. Then I saw a look in my father's eyes that I would never forget. It wasn't his fault. From that moment on, I knew that my father truly loved me, and I knew there was something wrong with my mother.

I was about 3 years old when this happened. We lived in a rural town in Michigan, in a trailer that sat on a wooded lot of 20 acres. I had a jungle-gym with a wooden slide that gave me my first splinter. I remember watching my father clear-cut part of the property with his chainsaw. When you're 2 years old and watching a tree get cut down, it's like watching a giant fall from the sky. The crackling and splitting of the wood, the whoosh that grows exponentially as the branches come crashing down: it's something magical.

I have many sweet memories of those times. I remember the love of my sisters, who cared for me, protected me. I remember my brother, who toughened me. Although they were half-siblings, if it weren't for their love, I might still be in a dark place.

It was during that time that I touched the exhaust pipe on the lawn mower. The memory is vague, but I recall my own screams to be saved. My father slept beside me the entire night, holding my hand in a bucket of water.

I also remember my father teaching me to cook eggs. I cracked one open while sitting on a stool that put me above the stove. I dropped the egg on the floor, as a 3-year-old should. My mother yelled at my father.

At night I would sometimes sneak into the dimly lit kitchen, open the refrigerator and pinch off nibbles of spinach, my favorite at the time.

I had a pet rabbit for a while. I don't remember what happened to that rabbit, but I also don't recall eating any odd-flavored soups. I remember laying on the couch with my mother as she watched Oprah. Those are my earliest memories and although they're very brief, they remain. And they are still real.

I was around 4 when we moved out of Harvey to Ishpeming, another small town in Michigan. My mother and I lived in a duplex near the Phelps elementary school. I'm not sure whether my mother had full custody of me or not, but I did see my father frequently. Many times, he came to pick me up in his 1979 Chevy pickup, and we'd go explore the woods, or to his landscaping job-site, or to play on the shore of Lake Superior. My father did a lot with me during that time – a lot. He'd also take me to various churches on weekends.

He was 'church hopping'. I didn't get the point – to me it seemed like a lot of different people getting together to play guitars and sing about God. I was too young to see what was happening. Now I can see that he was searching for something – searching for what, I don't know, but we all seem to have our voids, for whatever reason. I know I have mine, and I've seen myself trying to fill them in various ways.

Some parts of my childhood were incredible. We spent a lot of time on the road. One day, my father and I were driving down a back road, probably near Chatham. It was the middle of summer, the middle of the day. He sat me on his lap and let me steer the truck. We both laughed hard from joy and excitement. The sun glistening down through the maples that tunneled the gravel road.

Another day, when I was 4 or 5, my father took me on a hike to see a waterfall. I think it was Crystal Falls, I'm not sure. The fall was like a cylinder of heavy rain cast off a ledge about 30 feet high. My father walked beneath it with my hand in his, then picked me up with my back to the water and looked at me and smiled. He held me and we were soaked in what felt like a baptism of father-son bonding.

In winter, he would pull me on a sled through the woods. He showed me ice-caves in Eben, a place of magic. The nature, the love, the laughter: this was the heaven that every child deserves.

GREEN BAY

Living in Ishpeming for part of my childhood was all a boy could ask for. There were many kids to play with, school was in walking distance from home, and boredom hadn't been learned.

I often came home from school to a babysitter by the name of Linda, a very kind woman who was friends with my father. She took care of me in Ishpeming, or sometimes at her place east of Champion, near Koski's Corner. One day, she said, "Brandon, we're going on a trip, and you have two choices. Would you like to go to Disney World, or to Green Bay?"

I thought about it, and since I hadn't heard of Green Bay before, I replied, "Green Bay."

She said okay (and probably thought, "well that was easy") and we went to Green Bay. A place called Green Bay can sound pretty fantastic to a 4-year-old, let me tell you.

Coincidentally, it was during my fourth year I moved to Green Bay, Wisconsin. My mother had married a man who was a former high school teacher. She worked with Jenny Craig, and my new step-dad ended up selling used cars. We moved into a temporary apartment for about a week, then we settled into another apartment in that same complex.

My father stayed in Michigan, a four-hour drive away. Looking back, I can see the difficulty of his situation. The mother of his first child had moved across the country with his daughter, and now the mother of his second child left him following an affair. He was an honest, hardworking man, and everything he'd poured his heart and soul into left him at the flick of a dime. Perhaps it was even harder on him, knowing that his son only wanted to live with him.

Not too long after these events, my father found himself in a coffee shop reading National Geographic magazine. He came across an article about an artifact that that had been discovered in Egypt – a tithe receipt, dated back to around the time of Christ. On its inscription was the name Yahweh, written in ancient Hebrew. It was at that very moment that the only member of the House of Yahweh in the entire Upper Peninsula of Michigan approached my father with a brochure titled "The Creator Has a Name." That moment proved to be my father's calling. Coincidence or not, it was then that my father embarked on his path to the House of Yahweh.

Not long after my father's freak episode of synchronicity, I was riding with him in his truck.

I was around 5 years old at this time. We were riding down a back road, and I was in the passenger seat, watching the wind in the trees along the rural roads of Ishpeming. My father kept talking about Yahweh. I don't remember what he was saying, but I remember his excitement and obsessiveness. I still see the same sort of obsessiveness in myself at times, a multi-faceted quirkiness that might lead to a variety of outcomes.

"You're talking about Yahweh too much, Dad." I said. He shrugged and looked out the driver's-side window. "Yeah, well."

I visited my father about once a month. My mother had

custody, so it was up to him to come and visit me in Green Bay. Sometimes my mother would meet him half-way, but the drive was difficult for her, so my father covered most of the distance.

My life in Green Bay was nothing to complain about. The only down-side was not seeing my father as much as I would've liked. My step-dad was kind. He had a bad reputation for a bad decision he'd made, but no rational adult would've held it against him for long. Like any man, he had his vices, but he never treated me or my siblings poorly. I only have great memories of him, and I'm glad he was in my life.

Shortly after that first apartment complex in Green Bay, we moved to a duplex close to my babysitter's house. Like my earlier babysitter, her name was Linda, too. She was married and had two children, one of whom, her son Adam, would become my long-lost childhood friend. He was like a brother to me. Close to my age and incredibly talented in gymnastics, and similar to me in many ways. We were buddies, and I wonder about him to this day. His mother was ever so kind. I'll always have mixed feelings about babysitters, but Linda treated me like her own child.

My babysitter's house was in walking distance from a Hardees restaurant where my father sometimes took me. I met him there on my 6th birthday and soon became aware of the shift about to occur in my life.

My legs were hanging off the seat, kicking back and forth as I dipped French fries in ketchup. He handed me my present and said, "I don't want you to be upset, but this is the last birthday present I'll be giving you."

"Okay," I said, still concentrating on my food. Deep inside, I knew my father loved me, and that that wouldn't change.

It had been a month since his last visit. I unwrapped the gift and found a GI-Joe helicopter –pretty cool, and something I had wanted. "This doesn't mean I won't buy you presents anymore, Brandon. I just won't be getting them for you on certain days."

Shortly after that birthday, my father took me to a gathering place in Manitowoc, Wisconsin, where many from the House of Yahweh gathered each month for a special Sabbath Service. There I was introduced to the people, the customs, and the religion that would guide the rest of my childhood.

THE FIRST SABBATH SERVICE

Travelling to Manitowoc, Wisconsin, for Sabbath services was my next new experience.

The town was rural, and close to Lake Michigan. The congregation was centered around a farm where they grew potatoes. There weren't any neighbors close by; everything was fairly secluded. I didn't know what to expect, and I remember being a little nervous before we arrived. My father assured me that everything would be fine, that there were other children my age.

The first time my father and I went to Manitowoc, we went on a Friday night. Sleeping arrangements were made in the downstairs living room of a large house. The services were held upstairs, on Saturday afternoons.

There was another boy there, a little older than me. He was kind and had similar interests – bb-guns and baseball. He also had three older sisters. Everyone in his family was kind, and I felt very accepted into the group. They told me about another group of boys, who were brothers, and they suggested I might become good friends with the eldest, Edward. In fact, Edward and I were to become great friends throughout our time in the cult. Along with one of his best friends, Jake, we eventually became a trio in our shared deviance. Three 'alpha' males who stuck together.

I went to sleep that first night on a fold-out bed from a couch in the living room, and nothing seemed odd.

The next morning, we woke up and had a breakfast so healthy that everything tasted a bit like cardboard – but that was okay. I was eager to do something, to play, but we weren't allowed to do much. It was the Sabbath, the day of rest.

So I walked around and talked with Jim, the young boy I'd met the night before. He showed me around the farm grounds and soon Edward showed up, along with others there to attend the services.

We were about 40 in all. Everyone brought food – a pot-luck, though no one called it that. Soon enough, I'd learn about the words we weren't allowed to speak, and 'pot-luck' was among them. Of course I didn't know what a pot-luck was yet, so I was just excited that there was plenty of food and nice people.

Glass dishes full of lasagna, baked potatoes, coleslaw, served in a room perpendicular to the congregation area, which had folding tables with metal chairs set up. As my father and I found seats, the men and women were putting on their garments for worship. My father handed me a circular piece of cloth and told me to put it on my head. "It's a holy garment, we have to do this for prayer."

I placed it on my head, looked around and saw women with scarves over their heads, men with white linen sheets around their shoulders. We all stood to begin services.

"Will everyone please rise, and raise their hands for opening prayer," said the elder wearing a black Kippah (Yamika) and standing at the podium.

"Our heavenly father Yahweh…" The prayer began. Our heads were bowed, eyes closed or looking to the floor, hands raised and palms outward. This was the beginning of

15

the Sabbath service, a tradition I would keep for the next twelve years.

THE FIRST SET OF RULES

The trend began when I was 6. My mother had custody of me while we lived in Green Bay, but my father would pick me up each month to attend Sabbath services in Manitowoc. It seemed as if every time I visited, I learned more about the things that I needed to do, or couldn't do. This would continue throughout my duration in the House of Yahweh.

The dos and don'ts began with words I could or couldn't say, starting with my first visit. Someone would ask, "How are you today?" and I might respond, "I'm doing good." And they would say, "Oh, we don't say that word. It means God."

"So what am I supposed to say?" They would always have a set of other words to choose from – 'well', 'great', 'fine', 'blessed', 'joyous'… But 'good' was not appropriate.

We couldn't say 'happy', we couldn't say 'lucky', 'chance', 'fortune', 'weird', 'charm'. One elder once told me I couldn't say 'curious'. Right after it left my lips he said abruptly, "Shhh! don't say that, say 'inquisitive'."

We were also told not to use the days of the week, the names of the months, or the planets in the sky, because these were all named after various Gods. Shortly, all these words were removed from my vocabulary, and new words were put in their place. My mother didn't appreciate the new things that I was learning. She definitely thought it was "weird" – and it was, but I couldn't see it at that time.

All I really ever wanted was to live with my father, and

following the ways of the cult seemed like a worthy sacrifice.

I spent about a year in Green Bay. I attended a second year of kindergarten at McArthur Elementary and began the first grade there. During that year, we moved to Des Moines, Iowa, where I would finish the first grade. At that age, I started to learn more about the 'food laws' that the House of Yahweh promoted.

At first, the food laws might be viewed as rather healthy, very similar to Jewish food customs. They were reasonable in a cultish sense, although I was about to give up some foods that I did enjoy.

The first food off the list was pork – a big no-no. No bacon, no ribs, nothing with pork in it. Also no rabbit, bear, or anything unusual like that. Deer and cattle were okay. Mammals needed to have a split hoof, completely divided, and must also 'chew the cud'. Chicken, ducks, quail, and turkey were all fine, but no ostrich. Birds had to have both a crop and a gizzard. Fish or anything from the sea had to have fins and scales, so no shrimp, lobster, scallops, oysters, or the like.

Ingredients made these rules tricky. We weren't supposed to eat anything with pork in it, and that eliminated many foods from our grocery list – Jello, for example, which contained gelatin, was off the list. Tootsie rolls were another. Also eliminated were non-edible items such as shampoos that might have been developed with animal testing.

Looking back, it all seems ridiculous, but the word that

best describes the context is 'restrictive'. I was being groomed for an environment based on restrictions.

One to two times a month, I was bathed with teachings from the House of Yahweh, and I would take these teachings everywhere I went, be it my public schools or the dinner table at home. "I can't eat that because it's unclean."

The notion that I wanted to live with my father so dearly – coupled with the fact that he was deeply involved in a bizarre religion – upset my mother tremendously. However, it gave her grounds to start preparing for a future legal confrontation.

Despite learning these new rules to live by, I managed to have a childhood during this time. I was often able to play with children and get into typical shenanigans. But if I was an odd child to begin with, these new practices were only adding to my oddness.

THE COMPOUND IN TEXAS

I was about 7 years old when my father had me take a couple weeks off from school, to go to Texas. I was told there would be even more children down there, and that it was a lot of fun.

He had already been down once or twice. We were headed there to celebrate the feast of Tabernacles. There were three feasts a year that we had to attend in Abilene, and we would continue to do that for the next several years.

The drive was long. We drove in my father's pickup truck from Ishpeming, Michigan, to Abilene, Texas. Eventually, I got used to it. The actual grounds were about 25 minutes outside Abilene. It was similar to the distance from Ishpeming to Marquette in Michigan – except this town, Clyde, was literally in the middle of nowhere. A few thousand people, and the compound was definitely 'off the beaten path'.

A few left turns, one right onto a dusty gravel road, a few more rights and another left, and there we were at the gate. At that time I called the place 'the feast grounds', which makes it sound a bit nicer. It almost helped me ignore the barbed wire surrounding the 44-acre compound. Inside there were a few houses, very basic, three or four at the most. Some were just getting plumbing. There were a few trailers scattered about, a lot of RVs and campers, and a lot of tents. The heart of the compound was a tent city. I'd estimate that there were about a thousand people on the grounds at that time. The feast was almost ready to begin.

At the time, I felt that the people with whom I initially came in contact were genuine and kind. I still feel that way about most of them. Other children near my age were excited to meet me, as I was them. There was a basketball court over a dirt playing area, and a baseball field, and while all of these things were makeshift, they seemed to work well for everyone. Most people who lived on the grounds didn't have much money or many possessions. If they lived there, they worked for the House of Yahweh, and if they worked for the House of Yahweh, you can bet that grown men were working for wages as little as $3 an hour.

'Hurry! Hurry! Hurry! Work! Work! Work!' That was one of their mottos, and boy did they ever want us to work. There was always something to do, and if you didn't drop whatever it was you were doing for yourself, you felt shamed. My father, who was the hardest working man I ever knew, fit in well with this. I, on the other hand, had immense difficulty finding motivation, so there were times where I figured out ways to get out of it.

Most of the work was to move around buckets of food storage. We'd get a semi-truck loaded with 5-gallon buckets of food, and about 20 to 40 of us would move the buckets into stationary trailers, to store the food. This food was in preparation for the coming 'tribulation' (something that was supposed to have happened long before I left).

A lot of work was needed before the feast started. If it wasn't moving food storage, or helping to build another structure, it was helping older people to set up their tents. It was exhausting, and sometimes I was annoyed by it.

21

The feasts always started at sunset. There was a prayer and some form of services held at the sanctuary. The next morning, the men would get up around 6 a.m. and meet for men's prayer at 7 a.m. We would gather in circles of 3 to 6 and say prayers. After that, we would have breakfast, and then get dressed for services that started at 10:30, and these lasted roughly 2 hours. We'd have lunch in between, and then there would be another service at 2 p.m. Then (finally) the services would end around 4 p.m. At 7 p.m., the men would attend yet another prayer session, and at 8 p.m. there was often another class to attend. If there was any free time, we were to spend it studying or working.

Sitting for long hours in the sanctuary will teach anyone discipline. A hard metal folding chair surrounded by broad stretches of concrete was no place for a child who likely suffered from ADHD. At least at that time, my legs were short enough to swing from the edge of the chair.

Every feast day was like this. Long and rather boring, but filled with instruction, and every feast would bring new practices to our lives – either adding to existing practices, or finding flaws in previous ones.

All the members took part in correcting each other. "We can't say that," "We can't eat this." At this time, however, people were more relaxed than when I left, years later. A lot of people were 'hippie-ish' in their own way. Some even smoked a joint inside their tent here and there. Looking back, maybe that's why fewer people were so uptight in those early days.

Aside from the work and the long services for which I

had no attention span, I was able to make friends and find time to play. The only real struggle was the transition from this environment back to my mother's house and public school.

The year was 1992, and I was leaving the compound to attend the first grade in Des Moines.

At that age, a child can't be fully aware of the stress that he or she goes through. Drastic transitions aren't met by rational thought, but only by physiological responses. It seemed like every time my parents exchanged me, I would get sick, nauseous, and throw up. It was predictable like clockwork. Looking back, that was the only way my body was able to deal with those transitions. I was always anxious when passed between one parent and the other.

MOVED AGAIN

Before I started the second grade, we moved again, to the south side of Milwaukee. In Green Bay we had lived in two apartment buildings, and in Iowa we lived in an apartment building. In Milwaukee, we would live in a duplex near Jeremiah Curtin Elementary, where I attended the second and third grades.

People often refer to family dynamics, and my 'family' was sure dynamic. My mother, stepfather, and I stayed in the upstairs apartment of the duplex, while my stepfather's parents lived downstairs. This worked out conveniently for my mother, since my 'adopted' grandparents could watch over me when my mother and Jim went out at night.

I was very blessed to have them there. Not only were they kind, they were more understanding than my mother could ever know. I became sick at night often. It was around this age that I started having to deal with nausea and difficulty sleeping. Many nights, I had to get out of bed to vomit before I could sleep again. There were also nights where my mother handed me a pill and said, "Take this." I was too young to know about sleeping medication, but they knocked me out.

I lived in this duplex for about a year. It was in a nice neighborhood, with some children but mainly older people. Jim or my mother would give me a ride to school in the morning and then pick me up later. I remember seeing Bill Clinton one day when he visited Milwaukee. He drove right by my school.

This year in my life was when things started to feel more stable. School was situated nicely alongside my family life. My stepfather was kind, and my mother's work appeared to be going well. Even though I was attending the feasts three times a year, transitioning between the two lives didn't seem all that difficult.

I remember waking up one morning, and my mother told me that my cat was going to be put to sleep, and that I should say goodbye. I was mortified: I loved that cat. I was in tears nearly the whole day. I remember walking into Mrs. Zapnick's class with my head low, and when she asked, "Is everything okay?" I ran to my desk, put my head down and sobbed.

It was sad, but I was okay by the end of the day.

This was also the year that we would try to make the transition so I could live with my father. It was something I had wanted ever so dearly, since the age of 3. It's not that I felt that my mother was evil (I certainly don't look at it that way now), but for whatever reason, some people are damaged, and in certain situations, they can render themselves 'incapable'. In any case, I was ready to leave Milwaukee and move back to the Upper Peninsula of Michigan.

Between the monthly Sabbath gatherings and feasts with my father, my mother brought me to a child psychologist. He would ask me various questions while I played with toys in his office. I remember going to him several times. My mother told me that he said I was 'brainwashed'.

I didn't know what that meant, but my father would say that they were the ones who were brainwashed. Then, between the spring and summer of my second grade year, my mother took me to a doctor for an unexplained reason. I was asked to take off my underwear so the doctor could look at my testicles. I couldn't understand why, and I was very uncomfortable with the whole situation. My mother was standing behind me. She said something like, "We need to know that both of them are there." I said they were, but I didn't want to be touched – really, what little boy would want to be examined like that? In the end the doctor didn't touch me, but a conversation arose between him and my mother that would shape the next year.

Later in the summer, I moved in with my father, meaning I would start the third grade at North Lake Elementary. We were in a small neighborhood surrounded by woods, and the neighborhood boys were fun to play with. I'm not sure a young child could ask for more. My friends knew where I lived, and often on Saturdays they would come and ask if I could come out and play. My father would say no and tell them it was the Sabbath, as if they knew what that meant.

"You want to go out and play? Is it that important to you? More important than our heavenly father? You can't give up one day a week? Go out and play!" he told me once, trying his hand at reverse psychology. I stayed in that day and didn't go out to play until sunset.

Another odd thing happened this summer that led to catastrophe. My father wanted me to get a picture taken so I could eventually get a passport, in case we wanted to take a trip to Israel (or something). The day he decided to do this, it came completely all of a sudden: "Wake up, put your shirt on, let's go." The only time I'd had my picture taken before was for school, so of course I didn't like the shirt I was wearing, my hair was messy, and it all seemed poorly thought out. So I went, but a little disgruntled, and I wasn't shy about showing my emotions.

Within a few weeks, my father, stepmother, and I were at home in North Lake. A knock came at the door. It was the police. They were there for me – to take me away. Away from all that I wanted to be with, despite the weird religion and my father's odd quirks. They were taking me away. I walked out of the apartment and into the hallway. My mother was waiting around the corner.

Strangely enough, my mother and Jim took me to her first husband's house. I don't know why, but for a reason completely unrelated to what was going on. I could barely see through my tears. I didn't know why this was happening. My mother's ex-husband was there with his wife, my stepfather, and I believe my sister. None of this made sense to me, and as I looked at my mother's ex-husband's face, I could tell he was confused as to why I was so upset. My mother came to me and tried to hold me as I cried, but somehow I knew that this was all her doing. I pushed her away and I went to Jim, my stepfather, and he took me into his arms.

This was the beginning of a period of depression that would last for months. I was going back to Milwaukee, away from my father, once again.

Honestly – depression at age 8. It's hard to imagine, but I was down, and nothing could bring me up. My mother offered to buy me toys, to take me to places, but it simply wouldn't scratch the surface of my turmoil. Every time my father called me on the phone, the moment I heard his voice would bring me to tears. I felt cheated. We'd been cheated, and I honestly felt that I was living with the person who'd cheated me.

As it turned out, the reason I was taken away so easily was because the court system had been somehow manipulated; there was a 'theory' that my father, or someone, was molesting me. The doctor during that prior physical said that I was behaving like someone who had been molested. It still boggles my mind.

This was the very first deep wound that I would have to endure. It took months for me to get through. Even as I attended the third grade in Milwaukee, the first few weeks or months were filled with these difficult emotions. During this time, I also learned that my mother was tape-recording all conversations I had with my father. My father told me about it, and that the courts had ruled that she had to stop doing it. I pointed this out to her one morning while catching her listening to the recordings. She responded with anger and defensiveness, in efforts to take attention away from what she was doing. This type of response would become commonplace. Not only with my mother, but with my family and even myself. Freedom from guilt was a common goal among us. Shortly after catching my mother with these recordings, I would begin to witness my mother's third divorce.

Meanwhile, changes were afoot in the House of Yahweh. It was 1993, and teachings about multiple marriages were being issued from the pulpit and accepted by many followers. Most accepted the teachings, but some didn't and left. There were always at least a couple of people leaving every feast. The 'multiple marriage' thing didn't mean much to me. I was young, and whatever I was told was okay by my 'elders', I tended to accept.

The teachings about multiple marriages weren't that you had to have multiple wives, but merely that you could. There were a few men with more than one wife already. There was an elder from Maine who had a couple of wives. Yisrayl himself was known to have several wives, and there were a few other elders as well as non-elders and deacons with more than one wife.

ANOTHER DIVORCE

My stepfather had a drinking problem.

It was a problem I wasn't really aware of, and that didn't really affect me. My mother would point it out sometimes, saying, "Oh, Jim is drunk, don't go around him." As if she were trying to demonize him to me. But the truth is, though he might have been drunk, he was still kind, still jolly, and to this day I still don't feel it necessary to judge him. The only problem I saw was a bigger one: that his drinking was symptomatic of another unhealthy situation. His marriage.

I remember my father telling me when my mother married Jim: "Brandon, when I married your mother, your brother's dad told me she would do the same thing to me, and I said no, she had changed, she was different now. Well I told Jim the same thing, and he said the exact same thing that I had said." I vaguely remember responding, but not with much more than a shrug.

I was still depressed. Dealing with the distance from my father was something I didn't know how to bear. My mother and I moved again during this time, to an apartment building that was somewhat nearby, but closer to my elementary school. We were also closer to more children, so finding friends with whom to get into mischief wasn't difficult. There was a wooded area behind the neighborhood with a river running through where I would spend many summer days with my friends.

Although I had a diverse group of friends, and various activities to keep me busy in Milwaukee, this was a difficult year for me. Perhaps the difficulty and stress were mostly kept subconscious, since I wasn't able to rationally see what was happening around me. But looking back, this year shaped me tremendously.

As my depression faded, we settled in the new apartment and my mother showed behaviors that I hadn't before witnessed. I remember saying to my father, "She's acting like a teenager." I even remember saying something similar directly to her, and her cheerful response was, "That's exactly how I feel."

She liked to party, but I don't hold that against her. I remember one day, she and her date came home from a bar. I was on the floor with my friend playing video games. Her date tripped right over me, because he was so drunk. She laughed, and then they went to the bedroom.

Moments like these filled that year, and the times I got the 'I'm gonna be your new daddy' speech from random boyfriends and flings taught me a lot about how men can behave.

Looking back on all this, seeing these experiences through adult lenses, it's not difficult for me to feel compassion for my mother and other people who came in and out of my life. We all have moments of suffering, and who am I to hold that against anyone?

To top all this off, I was still travelling to Texas three times a year, and the House of Yahweh was still evolving its practices to become more strict and fundamentalist. This is when I started hearing the other children at school say, "Why don't you just move to Texas?"

I'd hear this phrase time and again until I left the cult. Something about me was changing, and I was starting to not be accepted by my peers. It was a feeling that I wouldn't really rationalize for another decade.

Toward the end of that year, Jim got in a drunk-driving accident and nearly died. Totaling his truck, he broke his back and ended up bedridden for many weeks. My last memory of him was when we went to pick up some belongings from his parents, and to say 'hello' and 'goodbye'. I walked into the living room and there he was, laying on the couch. I looked at him and I felt that something about him had changed. He had learned something – something real. His new lover was with him, taking care of him. It was nice to see him again, and I felt happy for him.

I walked down the flight of stairs toward the driveway separating the duplexes, and the sun was shining on the grey pavement. I walked to the car, opened the passenger door, and before I sat down my mother asked, "Was his new girlfriend there?"

"Yes" I said.

"Was she pretty?" She asked.

MEMORIES

I have a storm of memories from my childhood, until about the age of 10. I've already mentioned one vague, cloudy memory of my father showing me how to cook eggs. I was standing on a wooden chair, and my father cracked an egg and dropped it in a bowl to be scrambled. I cracked an egg and dumped it on the floor. My mother was in the living room, heard what happened and became very angry.

My impression of my mother at that age was that she was extremely concerned with keeping the apartment clean. Several times a week, when I was big enough, I'd scrub the kitchen floor or vacuum. We rarely had home-cooked meals, so the dishes didn't pile up much. In any case there was always a dishwasher.

I remember sitting in the grass outside of the green duplex, down the street from Phelps Elementary. I was no older than 4, and sitting on my butt like any child would. I looked to my right, and there on the ground were some mushrooms.

I was the type of kid to sneak in the kitchen at night and nibble on spinach, so mushrooms on the ground looked like food. Without hesitating, I grabbed a handful and ate them. My last memory of this situation was my sister running towards me screaming. She was afraid I was going to get sick, like when I'd gone into the bathroom and ate her medication. I can't remember what it was, but one day my sister and mother saw me leave the bathroom with white powder all over my face. They were scared for my life.

I was a brat! A brat who would grow into a smart-ass, and a smart-ass who would eventually get arrogant – but I'll get to that later.

Children mimic the behaviors of their parents, first and foremost. If not the parents, then whoever they spend the most time with. It might be teachers at school, or the television, or their siblings – what have you. What confused me most as a child was that when I behaved toward others the same way other people behaved toward me, I got scolded. I could never talk to my mother the way she talked to me. Logic was absent from these situations. My mother was generally the first person to notice this behavior, but it was often met with a wooden spoon, so not many others would see it.

The care and love that a boy gets from his older sisters is tremendously beautiful to me. I was once reminded by one of my sisters how my mother would carry a wooden spoon around in her purse to threaten me in public. I don't remember this, but it's not surprising. If you know me, I'm kind of different, because I come from 'different' people.

Back to my sisters: I had two older half-sisters. One from my father's side and one from my mother's side. These young ladies took care of me when I was a baby. Although they were young, they showed me all the love they possibly could, and it nourished me into adolescence. If it weren't for them, I might not be writing this.

I've expressed some difficult moments about the relationship between my mother and myself. But like I've said – sometimes, people are damaged. Regardless of the reason, this sort of damage can render one incapable. And for that, we cannot judge; if I see this sort of suffering in someone, I strive to find ways to be compassionate with them.

This compassion I get from my sisters, who likewise had a difficult relationship with my mother (perhaps worse than mine), and yet they were able to pick me up when I was a baby, and hold me, and speak to me gently, and turn any poison that they might have received into medicine for themselves, and for me.

Where would any of us be without love?

2. PRELUDE TO A CULT

It's difficult for me to talk about my childhood in the sense that I find it very hard to not make my mother look like a bad person. I have no intention of portraying her in such negative terms, but certain aspects of our relationship drove me to want to live with my father. Although I love her deep in my heart to this very day, I'm compelled to discuss certain moments of my past in detail, so the reader might better understand the decisions I made later in life.

When I was 9 years old I saw my mother playing the "dating game". It seemed as if man after man entered and left our lives. I didn't know what to think of it, though I don't judge my mother for it either. I knew there were many other problems in our lives, both individually and between us. She always struggled with an eating disorder. Along with that, she had fairly strict standards for aesthetic appearances, in people and in things. I meanwhile struggled with the line of fundamentalism that I would be brought into: the clash between who I was being molded into, and who I might naturally be. There was also a dissonance between my mother and myself, some failure in connection that I might never understand.

My relationship with my mother has played a part in how I would relate to nearly every woman I've been close to in life, and that was true at the House of Yahweh as well as after I left. I have many memories of my mother expressing anger, mostly when it was just her with her children. She seemed happy and likeable around anyone else. Then there's the time that we spent together, which wasn't much. Instead I spent time with babysitters, neighbors, or with the television when I was old enough. In some ways, my relationship with my mother was like watching someone's life that didn't really relate to mine at all.

My relationship with my father felt different. It was like music: either it felt good, or it didn't, and because I sensed honesty and compassion on his part, I was driven to be with him. Despite extended court visits, therapist sessions, and propaganda against the House of Yahweh, I still chose to live with him. I was entering a realm of darkness that would provide a lesson, filled with years of difficult intricacy.

I moved into my father's apartment in North Lake, Michigan, during the summer between the third and fourth grades. From then on, I would live with strict and evolving food diets, prescribed cleanses, daily practices ranging from prayer to the holding of a strict Sabbath. This is also when the teaching was revealed that Satan (or Lucifer) was a woman. The teaching went like this: Satan was at one time the wife of Yahweh, but she became disobedient, so Yahweh cast her out of heaven. I would also begin to learn about and to practice tithing – free-will offerings to the house of Yahweh – and to surrender myself completely to the teachings of Yisrayl Hawkins.

I will go on in detail about the house of Yahweh's strict regime of religious practices later, but what naturally happens when wholeheartedly entering religious fundamentalism at such a young age is a kind of dance between two opposing forces in life: the cult and public school.

BALANCING BEHAVIORS

I remember a time when my mother and I were visiting Ishpeming. We were staying at a hotel in the country village, and I remember swimming in the pool when my father and a lady walked up. She was a sort of care-taker that he'd met in the House of Yahweh, and he announced that they'd just got married. I couldn't believe it. I remember talking to my father about it later in the hotel room. I told him I was upset that he had planned on marrying her without telling me, like it was a secret. He described the situation to me, that she would be a great help around the house, and that he loved her, but he also needed her help.

Her name was Linda, and she was from Maine – China, Maine. Looking back, I don't think there could have been a more perfect woman for my father. She was hard working, kind and loving (under pleasant circumstances), and a great cook. I always look back on her cooking as simple, honest, hearty. This lady, along with my biological mother, would also have a significant impact on my life that would require years of understanding to unfold.

Before I lived with my father I knew that I was going to have to become a part of the House of Yahweh. We talked about it. I knew I was giving up my free time on Fridays and Saturdays, but I didn't know what all the repercussions might actually be.

I had been to Abilene, Texas, several times by then. Recently, we had driven a school bus from Manitowoc, Wisconsin, down there. My father bought the bus from

40

some of our friends there, also from the House of Yahweh. It was already partially converted to a camper-style setup. It was likely from the 1970s, white with blue and black stripes running down the sides. It had one of those old-fashioned levers that the driver would grab onto to open the door for passengers. It was cool, it was quirky, and it was our new dwelling-area for feast time.

The year must have been 1994, the summer before the fourth grade. I was living with my father and my stepmother in North Lake. We stayed in the largest building in the area owned by a local family named Gravedoni. The neighborhood was small and kids could probably ride every street of it in half an hour on their bicycles if they tried. We were surrounded by forests, miles of trails, wooded or fielded. It was and still is a beautiful area: so beautiful, it took me many years of seeing other terrains to appreciate it this way. Many of the trails started behind Northlake Elementary school. If you went far enough, you'd reach a rope swing that would take you about 40-feet off the ground, suspended by two big red pines with empty beer cans scattered around their roots. There was even an old car from the '20s or '30s buried in the woods. How did it get there? We always wondered.

Growing up in these woods and seeing random moss-covered rotting cars like that was the norm. Looking back, maybe one was dropped off by one of Al Capone's goons, back in the day. You never know, but that leads me to my next point.

At that age, and in the environment I was growing up

in, I needed fantasy – I needed escape – and I was able to find some through music, school, and deviance.

Mr. Stetson was my fourth grade teacher, and I gave him a hard time. As a matter of fact, I gave all my teachers a hard time. I might even say it got worse and worse until I was a junior in college.

I showed up to school early every morning to kick the soccer ball around in the gym. I also stayed late after school every day to kick the ball around some more. A couple of times, Mr. Stetson would come and play with me. He'd ask, "How come you're not going home?" I never really had an answer, but the truth was, I didn't want to be there. There was something about home that I didn't want to be around, although at the time I was completely unaware of it. My body just "responded", just has my behavior did. My functioning was completely subconscious at that age. Sometimes, it resulted in a physiological response of nausea and vomiting (every time I changed hands between my mother and father, vomiting arose like clockwork).

A lot happened for me during the fourth grade. Despite the different family atmosphere and different forms of (subconscious) stress, I did feel more at home. All my peers were nice, for the most part, and I developed a crush on a girl that would last for well over a decade. My father and I drove past her as she was running with the track team from Westwood High. There was something special about Amber, and to this day, everyone who knows her knows the same.

I officially dove into music at this time as well. I had a

toy saxophone when I was a toddler, and I loved to play it. I also fiddled with the guitar. But one day, my dad's friend Yeremyah, the only other member in the House of Yahweh outside of our family that lived in the U.P., stopped over and gave me a silver-plated saxophone made in the 1940s. It was passed between my father and him, and they couldn't really get a sound out of it. But when they handed it to me, I got a tone, and shortly after I was referred to as a natural, although I didn't really know what that meant.

Show-and-tell was fun the next day. The kids all called me Bill Clinton (also known to play sax), and Mr. Stetson also called me a natural. That day that he said that, a friend of mine carried my saxophone case back home for me, so I could play as we walked.

Perhaps the universe was looking out for me. Had I not been given that instrument, my life would be completely different. It was my biggest means of escape during that time, and again, I wasn't even aware of it.

The fourth grade provided many memories along with friends who would be with me all my life. Isaac the genius, how could anyone forget him? A man of logic who was in some way a team player and soldier in the battle I would face years down the road. Both he and his family were there for me when I needed them. I might say music and deviance defined this time period. I was always getting in trouble at school. Family life wasn't easy. Shortly after I moved in with my father and my stepmother, Linda and I began to fight continuously – a trend that wouldn't stop.

STRAINS OF DEVIANCE

Back when I was about 5 or 6 years old, my mother had taken me to the Milwaukee zoo. I was playing soccer with another boy who I'd just met. It was a hot day, and we were next to a pond, surrounded by picnic tables and people eating. I saw this boy standing next to the edge of the pond and I got a sudden urge to push him in the pond. I don't know what gave me that impulse, but I acted on it. Right after, I ran and hid behind a garbage can where my parents could obviously see me. The poor boy's mother pulled him out of the pond, and he was covered from head to toe in mud, or else that Milwaukee sludge that makes you wonder what those giant, mutated gold-fish really are.

I had a similar moment at North Lake elementary school, where I saw a boy named Chris playing next to a very large puddle. I pushed him in. Was it my sense of humor? I'm not sure, but I wish I had a nickel for every time my mother or sister told me I was a brat.

In some way, I feel that I've always been deviant. When someone sees logic in something, and an authority figure isn't adhering to that logic, then any loudmouth will question the authority, perhaps as they should. But with me, it was something else. There was a lot of pressure at home. Every morning, I would wake up, put my holy garments on, make breakfast, pray over the breakfast, fight with my stepmother over something meaningless, wait for dad to get home from the night shift, at which time things would settle down, and then I'd go to school.

It was a big transition from home to school every day. I had a fairly strict diet at home, and whenever there was pepperoni pizza at school, or something similar that someone offered to share with me, I had to refuse. When I was asked why, the only response within reach was, "Because it's unclean." Of course no one understood this. When you're different at this age, kids don't like you, or at the very least you're chastised.

A few days each week I left school and headed home with a feeling of dissonance, similar to the feeling I'd get when I made the transition between being with my mother and my father. I never had that feeling when spending time with my friend Edward and his younger brothers. Of course I didn't recognize the feeling as 'dissonance' but as a tingling in my teeth. A form of anxiety.

Edward (pseudonym) was more or less my age. I would see him every month in Manitowoc. He lived in a farmhouse in a very rural area beside a small park, a very beautiful area, and many afternoons we spent walking through the woods. We would also share our deviant characteristics. If we were together and it wasn't the Sabbath, we'd be playing with bb-guns, fireworks, knives, you name it, and this was the area to do it. Many people in the house of Yahweh from this area were ex-members of a militia group. Even one of the elders was considered the right-hand-man of Jimmy Wickstrom, leader of the Michigan Militia. So some of these people had some heavy artillery at their disposal.

Of course when you're a 10-year-old boy and you see a

45

chain of 50-calibre shells, you think it's pretty cool.

Edward and I got along well, though we had completely different lifestyles. He was homeschooled, while I wasn't. He was (truly) rural, and I wasn't. Hell, he barely knew how to work a television then, much less a game-boy, so it was funny watching him play Mario Kart back then. When he banked his turns, he'd be nearly lying on one side of his body. I said. "Ed, leaning doesn't help you turn any better."

Ed had a tough father, or maybe he was just tough at times. I remember one winter day, Ed and I had made a little fire out in the woods, just for something to do. His father found out and got so mad, he nearly picked up Ed by the throat as he slammed him against a wall. It wasn't the first time this happened.

In the House of Yahweh, the "rod of correction" was just that. Poor behavior was met more or less with violence. I was also subject to it one day. My father asked me to wind up my controller cords when I was done playing my video games. He said, "What if someone trips on it and breaks your machine?"

"I'll just buy a new one." I replied sarcastically.
"That's it, get upstairs." My father went to the fridge to grab a willow branch that he kept behind it – literally the "rod of correction." I was already crying before he beat me. I could swear I heard it whistling through the air before it met my bare-behind, leaving welts, cuts, and a little blood. Looking back, I feel sorry for my father for doing that. He was confused about how to go about disciplining a child, and the house of Yahweh more or less encouraged such

behavior from him, but shortly after, he regretted it deeply. He never hit me like that again.

Over the summer between the fourth and fifth grades, my family moved across the street into a triplex. There we had our own backyard and a basement, and more space in general. Looking back, maybe it was just more space for my stepmother and me to fight and argue, where the neighbors couldn't hear us as well.

UNCLEAN UNTIL SUNSET

It seemed the older I got, the more Linda and I fought with each other, and the more violent it became. The things we fought about were frivolous. Where the cereal box goes, which pan to use to cook eggs, etc. It didn't really matter what it was, there was always pent-up energy to be released by means of yelling and throwing things.

The cult was very hard on women, even back in 1995. There was a lot of psychological and emotional control over them, more so than over the men. For instance, when a woman is on her period, she's considered unclean until sunset. Not only is she unclean, but in the House of Yahweh's view, everywhere she sits also becomes unclean. So they carry around a placemat to sit on, as well as a notepad to leave a message wherever they sat: "Unclean until sunset." Women were unclean until a week after the last sign of blood, and they couldn't be with their husbands at this time. Luckily for the husbands, they could get extra wives.

Women in the House of Yahweh were the care-takers for the houses. They were responsible for everything: the cooking, the cleaning, buying groceries, taking care of the children. Also, they were the protectors of the home while the husband was out earning money. My father worked two jobs, so he wasn't home for 16 hours on most days. He worked hard. It's crazy to look back and see how much he worked. Some years, he made great money for someone who lived in Ishpeming. Sadly, however, about 30% of all his income before taxes went to the cult, thanks to tithes and free-will offerings. What I realized later, is that tithing in general is a preventative measure for the cult. People who invest their money into a cult are less likely to leave as time goes on.

So my father was often out working, and Linda was at home doing the duties expected of her. On top of all the work she was responsible for (truly a lot, and she did it well), she had to study the teachings of the cult, day in and day out. It was beaten into our heads: "Wives, submit to your husbands. Husbands, submit to the overseer, and children, submit to your parents." Submission was a big message, and another was: "Do not doubt the teachings of the House of Yahweh." We needed faith. Constantly.

Just as my forms of subconscious escape were music and deviance, which would continue to develop over time, my stepmother's form was to yell, scream, and throw things. Don't get me wrong, I fought back. Even though at times I realized that it didn't make sense, I fought too. Sometimes it got bad.

The kitchen was the worst place to fight. Knives were there, and when a 10-year-old child sees a knife go whizzing by him in the morning, it sets the mood for the day. Or being grabbed out of nowhere, and shaken. Having my clothes torn because of this. And the saddest part is that she would have never behaved that way, had she not been subjected to so much control herself.

I look back on this and I see it as a subtle form of "pecking order". There was literally no place for her to release any negative energy. Nowhere. So if any little thing bothered her, and if it came from someone under her authority, she would have to say something about it.

Despite our fights, we had moments where we enjoyed each other's company. Although we were both capable of fighting like we did, Linda still did an amazing job taking care of the house, and those home cooked meals are something I'll always be thankful for.

When I was young, my father, stepmother, and I would get together in the living room and watch television, or a movie. The nights were generally more easy-going. Although we'd sometimes fight at night, it happened mostly in the mornings. One night, the three of us were watching television and there was some cream soda sitting on the kitchen counter. I asked my father if I could have some, and he said, "You can only have one glass." It was a little unusual for him to limit it, so I went along and proceeded to fill up the glass right to the rim. It just made sense to me. I walked into the living room sipping out of the cup. My father looked over at me and said, "You filled that right to the rim? Why did you do that??"

I looked at him and thought to myself (or maybe mumbled out loud), "Why wouldn't I?" Then my stepmother said, "When you fill a glass, it's full at this point." And she pointed to the spot she thought was appropriate. I pointed to another spot on the glass and said, "What about here? Is that okay?"

We didn't fight that night, but I certainly was a little shit at times.

CHILDREN & SUPERSTITION

While I was moving between parents I often got sick – vomit and nausea like clockwork. I seemed to be always throwing up as a child. I remember being in the third grade, sitting on a toilet seat in my underwear late at night, crouched with my arms around my stomach. I would lean back and forth and play a game in my head: I would tell myself that for every second that I didn't throw up, I would gain "points", and those points would help me not to throw up. This eventually turned into a practice where I believed that if I thought of something bad hard enough, that it wouldn't happen. This invented game of superstition led to years of anxiety that wouldn't be unraveled until two decades later.

In the House of Yahweh, we were taught to have nothing to do with politics. Basically, this made it a sin to vote. Well when I was in the fifth grade, we had a mock election where we pretended to vote for a president. I was friends with a boy named Bobby, the popular kid. He and his brothers would be popular all through high school. Good athletes, good people.

Anyway, Bob Dole was on the ballot, and just for fun, Bobby's friends were voting for Bob. Something kids do, right? So I voted, and I knew I was going to have to hide it from my parents. When I got home they asked me what went on, and of course, I lied about it. I told them that I didn't take part.

You see, anytime during class where they were doing

anything that related to holidays, religion, politics, or even reading from a book that talked about these things, my parents told the teachers that I had to leave the class because it was against my religion. I tried to avoid such situations because of the chastisement I would receive later from my peers.

After I lied to my parents about voting, my stomach didn't sit well, and later that night I became sick. It might have been the flu, or stress, or both, but the next morning at 7:20 a.m. I was vomiting bile. I was terribly sick. Linda stood behind me as she watched me purge several times. She said, "Maybe if you go to school you'll feel better." I didn't have the energy to argue or fight. I let her dress me in the outfit she preferred that day, and I walked the 400 yards to school. When I got there, I sat down and didn't move until lunch time, when the teachers told me I needed to go home. Since I was often a jolly and loudmouthed brat, the teachers knew when I was honestly ill. That was the last time I threw up during my childhood years. In fact I've never thrown up again since then, except because of food-poisoning.

I look back now and perceive my stomach issues as a response to anxiety. It was just at this point that my anxiety would find another outlet. Although I'd still feel my gut turning during stressful times, now my teeth would tingle during moments of angst. Maybe it was at this time that I started to develop my habit of bruxism (teeth grinding), long before it was actually noticed. However, there was some type of relief that followed, in knowing that the days of holding my stomach while rocking my body back and forth on the toilet seat, chanting "don't throw up, don't throw up.." were likely over.

HOLLOW HOLIDAYS

Holidays still existed, but they had an essence of emptiness. When my father told me on my 5th birthday that it would be the last birthday for which he'd buy me a present, I was okay with that. One winter in North Lake, when I was about 11, Christmas was just around the corner. In school, whenever we were supposed to do anything related to a holiday, I had to leave the area. No singing Christmas carols, no eating Christmas cookies, no sharing gifts or anything like that. For some reason, I was more or less okay with it. The only thing that seemed to bother me was the fact that the other children didn't accept me for being different.

I was in the fifth grade, and my mother had left some gifts in a plastic bag outside my house, hanging on the entrance door. She'd come up from Milwaukee to visit her children. My father told me I needed to give back the gifts. It was clothes, mainly, and I didn't want to give them back. I wanted my gifts, but I was given a guilt trip by my father and stepmother.

Around that time I really became interested in music. I got all my toys together (Ninja Turtles and X-Men) and took them to a pawn shop and traded them for instruments. Music was going to become a type of blanket for me, and maybe shedding those toys represented some form of leniency toward my father.

Holidays would always pose complications in their yearly "waves". Holidays came and went, just as feast days came and went. Holidays can be stressful for anyone, but I had a little additional or at least different type of stress associated with them. My peers at school couldn't understand my special situation, and my siblings couldn't understand it, and my mother hated it. Through the Holidays she found ways to work with these traditions, which was probably a good thing.

Aside from holidays, I was shut off from a lot of things that a child would normally experience. At the same time, down in Texas, I was exposed to many things that some would never be exposed to. The things that I was closed off from posed complications later in life, thanks to mental blocks placed by the House of Yahweh. Mind control really did happen – it really is real. And it's easier for kids to get wrapped up inside it when their parents are leading the way.

All fundamentalist cults use similar ways of controlling their members, playing on their struggles and providing a means of relief while selling them a make-believe idea that they'll inherit something incredibly grand in the afterlife, if they just have faith. These poor individuals are then separated from family members who don't join them in their faith through the removal of old traditions. This includes holidays and any other family events that might take place. In the House of Yahweh, members are convinced that Satan will use their family members to try to persuade them to leave the House of Yahweh, so it's best to stay away from them all together; and above all, one must never, ever talk to family members who are no longer part of the House of Yahweh.

Once the House of Yahweh enables the separation of the members from their worldly ties, they are able to work in other means of control, eventually covering a very wide range.

Finances, thought processes, food diets, and all daily activities are influenced by the House of Yahweh. There's no getting around it, and at this time, in the early to the mid '90s, I remember the level of fundamentalism starting to drastically increase. Along with the increase in fundamentalism came an increase in money that the House of Yahweh was drawing from its followers.

We had tithes to pay, essentially 10% of our income, and any increase (be it a gift or inheritance) before taxes, got paid directly to the cult. Another 10% was required to get us to and from the feasts, and again, anything left over was supposed to go to the cult. Some years, yet another 10% was demanded by the cult. On top of this, the House of Yahweh sold food on the feast grounds, and since we were never allowed to leave the grounds during feast time, we had to buy our food there. In 1995, those food prices went up, and everything became very expensive. Not only that, but we had to buy supplements – essential oils by Young Living – and these prices were also inflated. Because these products were "blessed" by the priests, we had to buy them from the House of Yahweh.

HALE BOPP AND THE OKLAHOMA CITY BOMBING

The first five years in the cult were strange indeed, but nothing that would make most people worry. It was around the time of the arrival of the Hale Bopp comet that rather "spooky" teachings started to come over the pulpit from Yisrayl Hawkins and his minions.

In the mid '90s, during the feasts in Texas, an elder by the name of John Bragg or Yachanan Hawkins (his Hebrew name) compiled some videos about aliens, outer space, and conspiracies. These included snips from the Cosmos series by Carl Sagan, television dramas like The X-Files and similar videos. These were intended to persuade the congregation to believe that extraterrestrial life-forms existed, but that they were in fact a manifestation of Satan.

Here's the scoop on Hale Bopp: when that comet passed close to Earth, a lot of teachings and "prophecy" came out about how Satan was going to pass by on some sort of "star ship" and then be cast down to Earth to perform her evil in the last days leading to "tribulation". When another group of cultists committed suicide in California, and it was broadcast on the news, Yisrayl Hawkins said that in the future, those people would indeed be brought back to Earth on a space-ship to prove to the rest of the world that they were the way to salvation. He said that this is how Satan would gain many followers, and how it would potentially entice us to follow them, if we weren't strong with Yahweh's 613 laws.

The House of Yahweh had rented a very large telescope to look at the comet from the compound. It was the biggest I had ever seen, about 3 feet in diameter and 6 or 7 feet long. After people looked at the comet some would say how scary it was, and others would joke about seeing aliens walking around on it. Then teachings of fear really started to come down.

We'd been shown the footage of the Dave Koresh compound in Waco, Texas, destroyed by Federal forces, and we were told that the government might come some day, too, and try to destroy the House of Yahweh. That perpetuated the desire to buy more food storage, and to prepare to build underground bunkers in years to come. We were also encouraged to study the Holocaust. We were told on many occasions that something similar would happen to us, and that we needed to be prepared to die for what we believed in. It's hard to count how many times I've seen the movie Schindler's List – at least a dozen times.

I remember one feast when I made it to Texas and the Oklahoma City bombing of a Federal building had just taken place. "This is a sign that tribulation is around the corner!" Yisrayl Hawkins said. Around this time, the "world was supposed to end" – in 1997 or 1998 – so we needed to prepare. This strengthened everyone's resolve to continue buying food storage, to follow the laws more closely, and to continue paying tithes and giving more free-will offerings. Paying one's tithes was definitely one of the most important things to do in the House of Yahweh, if not The Most Important.

As greater fear of the End Times spread through the House of Yahweh, the degree of fundamentalism started to grow. The followers grew more likely to look at others and to point out their flaws, and they were more likely to be defensive about their own behaviors. Their insecurities grew along with their tendency to point fingers. This paranoia was an excellent platform for working more strict guidelines into people's lives. Perhaps this is where the curve in "growth in fundamentalism" really started to rise. That curve would never decline or plateau, and eventually it led to my disgust with the group and encouraged my definite separation.

LEARNING ABOUT MARRIAGE

Driving to Texas was a long trip. The hot stickiness of vinyl seats in Oklahoma were a reminder that we were only about 10 hours away. Arriving at the compound was always filled with mixed feelings. We'd arrive at the gate and talk to a couple guards who would inspect the vehicle a little bit before we were let in. This was generally a quick process. After we got in, the first thing I would always want to do is get out of the truck and walk to our campsite, and along the way I would always see someone I knew. "Shalom", we would say to greet each other.

Our campsite had that old school bus parked on it. Before we got our second camper, I would stay in a 6-person tent across the gravel road, on the edge of what was called "tent city". Tent city was probably the size of a soccer field. Telephone poles were laid on the hard ground and numbers painted on them to mark out the tent sites. The ground was a reddish clay that got really slick when it rained, and we had to dig trenches around our tents to keep the water from flooding them. There were times I would wake up to what seemed a river of water running underneath the tent. Sometimes it rained pretty hard, and everything became a muddy mess. Occasionally, someone would slip and get covered in mud, but at the very least our feet were covered in it.

The children played with other children of a like age group. Sometimes, an adult would step in and tell us how to improve our behavior to become more righteous. Some of the children went along with this more than others. When I was about 13, I remember some guys who came from the North-east, in their late teens or early twenties. They showed up on their own, with their own curiosity and ambitions. Some only came for two or three feasts, others stayed a while longer, and some didn't leave until after I left. But they all left eventually.

The tithing law seemed to be the most difficult to follow for the young men. It was the most important thing to do in the House of Yahweh, according to both Yedidyah and Yisrayl Hawkins. Yedidyah was an elder for many years, who eventually wound up in prison (more about that later). The young men had their own struggle. They were encouraged to work, often for low wages, to pay tithes, and to build their character, so that one day they would be suitable for a wife; which is what many of them wanted. So there they were, trying to get ready for such things, and then they would see the elders denying them communication with women, while the elders themselves take on these young ladies as second, third, or fourth wives. They wouldn't shun the men entirely, because they wanted their tithe money (or at least I think it's safe to say so). Marriage for the young men there was like the idea of salvation for everyone: "Eventually it will come."

Around this time I started to become aware of the marriage situation in the House of Yahweh. I didn't yet have any strong opinions on marriage, but I did see that the situation wasn't normal. The overseer had many wives at that time – many. We weren't encouraged to talk about it, because the information needed to be kept quiet, to protect the legality of the situation. On paper it looked like affairs, and the House of Yahweh didn't recognize any marriage outside the cult.

In a certain light, maybe I can make sense of a multiple marriage, like where three or four people just happen to come together and create a mutual agreement among themselves. Maybe that could be something. It's not for me, but I'm okay with keeping my nose out of a situation like that. The thing that really bothered me about the marriages in the House of Yahweh, especially among the elders and the leader, Yisrayl Hawkins, is that when a woman or girl marries Yisrayl, they get a "free ticket" into the kingdom of heaven. This is how they're encouraged to join in marriage as a second or third wife. I think it's safe to say that young girls around the age of 15 are easily manipulated in a situation like this.

Being that I was only about 13 when I started to really learn of these things, my opinions continued to be vague at best. I had ideas for what I felt might be appropriate for me, but there were other things to focus on. I remember becoming really sad around this time, and I wasn't the only one, and I didn't know why. I became sad for no apparent reason.

RESPONDING TO STIMULI

Sadness began to grow. I couldn't tell why, but there was an emotion inside me that could always bring out tears. I was in the compound, near the food court area, which was basically two semi-truck trailers that were up on blocks. They had staircases built up to them, and we would walk through while getting food served to us. And there were a couple of other stores located in these trailers, a toy store and a candy store.

One day, I was walking away from the sanctuary toward my campsite, and I crossed the food court only to find a girl sitting on the steps to one of the trailers and crying. She was older than me, about 15 or 16. As she cried, people stood around her, mainly her friends, trying to comfort her. Somehow, I could empathize with her emotions. I was told by one of her friends to move on, and so I did. I walked back to my tent and started to feel similar emotions work their way out of me.

I couldn't get it, and I didn't know why, but I was sad, and sometimes I would just cry. I told my father, and he would ask me why, but I had no answers. It was something that really stumped him. A few days later, I saw the girl who was crying, and I asked her what was wrong. She said she didn't know.

I look back on this, and it reminds me of the pecking order in the House of Yahweh's hierarchy. The pecking order was perfectly apparent, but its effects were more subtle, and I see this emotional response from children as something similar. With the rules and regulations being so strict in the religion, it makes sense that children would so respond to their surroundings, simply because it's a big shift from what anyone might be used to.

At that age, my deviance really began to grow stronger in my life. My friends in the cult, Ed and Jake, would share in this deviance. Before I begin a story of young boys trading Playboy magazines, I want to tell another story of something that happened when I was 10 years old.

For some reason, I never felt like I had privacy, mainly because of my stepmother. Occasionally she would make it known that she had gone through some of my things. I didn't like that, so I needed to figure a way where I could be sure that they wouldn't find my things, or at least my secret things. So I grabbed my Bible off the shelf and I spent an hour cutting pages out with my Swiss army knife. This would provide just enough space to house my secret belongings (which would eventually amount to a cassette tape from my brother, and girls' phone numbers, and that's about it). I cut into pages of the bible because I knew that would be the last place anyone would look.

YOUNG BOYS

Of course I don't have any shame in admitting a childish desire to look at pornographic magazines. I think curiosity is natural, and at a young age, purely innocent. How those activities are fostered over time, however, can determine much more. In the end, it's all childish behavior.

My friends and I had exchanged Playboy magazines for a while, between the three of us. I'm not sure how we got most of them. I think I got a few from a friend at school, who stole some from his dad. I'd bring them to Texas where the three of us would meet up, and Jake and Ed and I would exchange them and crack jokes about them. It was deviant, exciting, and something to pass the time between services (what most people would understand as Bible studies).

When it came time to hide those magazines (we generally had to hide many things, if they didn't closely parallel the HoY teachings), Jake had the great idea of taking an old magazine cover and taping it to the Playboys. I had the idea of keeping them in a plastic slip, which I had in my binder from school. This is how I ended up storing my 5 or 6 magazines. Then I found the perfect cover, and Jake and Ed thought it was pretty funny, and perhaps a little wrong.

In the House of Yahweh, we had this magazine-size booklet that was titled "The 613 Laws of Yahweh", and it turned out that the cover of that booklet fit perfectly around a Playboy magazine. When Ed and Jake saw that, they both laughed, and I remember one of them saying, "I'm not sure you should do that." My own thoughts on the issue were, "I don't want my parents to find these."

In the House of Yahweh, such behavior was a sin because it was taking part in the exposure of nakedness, and it also created lust. Unfortunately, I can't remember the photographs in those magazines, so there's definitely no lust left, but this was the reasoning for why it was wrong. We knew that if we were ever caught, we would have to be counseled by the elders.

My mother, on the other hand, as zany and cold as she could sometimes be, was very open with her sexuality and with the nudity of others. She wouldn't have seen a problem with me looking at Playboy. I even remember hearing her say so, although she also said, "No, he can't look at Penthouse, that's too hardcore." Had I not been in the cult, I believe that with my mother's attitude, and perhaps some guidance, my fascination with pornography would have faded much earlier than it did. I didn't realize it at the time, but there were men in the House of Yahweh who were perverts and pedophiles. Eventually, an elder would get arrested for this, but he wasn't the only one. Many men loved the idea of multiple marriages, and men often pursued young girls for marriage. Girls as young as 14 being pursued for marriage was not uncommon. And I do believe that being surrounded by this energy influenced not only my interest with pornography, but that of other young men in the cult as well.

Eventually one of us got caught, and it was Jake, whose

father was an elder. He yelled and screamed at Jake until he told on me and Ed. Or at least that's what Jake said to us when we all saw each other again at the next feast. I remember my father getting off the phone with the elder and coming to me saying, "Give me the magazines, where are they?" I went and grabbed my binder and pulled them out. He was surprised by how they were hidden. When he saw me pull the magazine out of the HoY cover he said, "I don't think you should keep that in there. Why did you put that in there?"

I told him "Because you wouldn't have looked there." He took the 5 or 6 magazines, including the 40-year special edition, and put them in a paper bag. The last I ever saw of them was the paper bag sitting on his bed, in his bedroom.

SEDAR AND ALCOHOL

There were three feasts a year that everyone needed to attend in Texas. The feasts of Tabernacles, Passover, and Pentecost, which happened in the fall, spring, and late spring, respectively. During the Passover, we had what was called the Seder meal, or gathering. It took place the night after what we called "Yashuah's Memorial". The memorial service was a solemn night that was a walk-through of Yashuah's death (Yashuah being the son of Yahweh, like Jesus is the son of God). It was like watching the "Passion of Christ" with a bunch of sad people. We would pray and wash each other's feet. It was very symbolic of the Bible.

The next night was practically party night for everyone. I recall the elders always warning to refrain from drunkenness on this night, and understandably so. We would drink eight glasses of wine during the ceremony, and the first time I took part I was 10 years old.

We were all gathered in the sanctuary, and folding tables were set up in rows that spanned about 100 feet. The floor plan to the sanctuary was about half the size of a football field. It was a very large cement area with steel I-beams to hold up the roof. There were hundreds of people gathered together to take part, and we were all dressed up, all excited, and all ready to joyously take part in the alcohol and food.

The ceremony went like this: we would all read in unison from a pamphlet and drink a glass of wine whenever the pamphlet instructed us too. My father wasn't filling my glass all the way, but I sure was getting my share of Kosher wine, Mogen David or Manischewitz. Towards the end of the ceremony I started to get very tired, and I ended up falling asleep at the table. To this day I can still hear my stepmother's words, "You were drunk."

I look back and still think it's a little funny, although I'm drinking scotch as I write this; I'm not sure if there's a correlation or not. The funny part was how we participated in a night like that, although drunkenness was a big sin. No one seemed to have a straight answer on what actually represented "drunk". Some would say, "Two beers! You can't have more than two beers." Another might say, "If you feel it, you're drunk." And then another would say, "If your thoughts are altered..." There was no clear definition, and I think that had a profound influence on how alcohol would affect me later in life.

I started drinking wine regularly with my father around the age of 12. Every Friday night, we would share a bottle of wine with dinner, and sometimes after dinner, we would have a night cap that was usually liquor.

As I drank like this, I always kept myself in check. I constantly wondered to myself, "Am I drunk?" Looking back, there were times where I clearly was, but somehow I was able to act sober. There were times when the room would move if I moved my head, or when my face was numb. Somehow, my behavior was never recognized as drunkenness, and I think this had to do with being raised somewhat "appropriately" in terms of alcohol (at least as seen in some countries).

With all that being said, I don't necessarily encourage

anyone to raise their children like this. I can just say that even through college, I never blacked out or had a D.U.I. or fell out of my chair. But the Seder was my first true experience with alcohol, and I barely remember it.

PUPPY LOVE

When my father gained custody of me, there was an agreement between my parents that I would visit my mother during the summer. She was a teacher and had summers off, so it worked out conveniently. She lived on the south side of Milwaukee around this time, near St. Luke's Hospital off 27th Street. I had a few friends there, and we'd often run around the city together, struggling to stay out of trouble.

I was 13 when I met Christine, at a McDonald's. It wasn't quite 'love at first sight', but not too long after meeting her I became deeply infatuated, and soon I was spending most of my time with her. We went to the movies for our first date. I can't remember what movie we saw, but it may have been 'The Sixth Sense'. My mother gave me money to go on this date: she said that I had to pay for everything and get Christine whatever she wanted. I thought this was a little unusual, because my mother rarely gave me money. It seemed she really wanted me to spend time with a girlfriend. She also gave me a lot of privacy with Christine, and a lot of freedom. Perhaps more than most parents would give their children.

On the other hand, I was not allowed to date anyone. Having a girlfriend in the House of Yahweh was a big no-no. Fornication was a huge sin, and anything leading up to that was just as evil. So dating was a secret that I'd have to hide from my father and stepmother. My mother helped me to keep it secret for a while; looking back, she did a lot to keep us together.

I really liked Christine. Somehow, we got along well, maybe thanks to our age, and our shared background – she had a bit of Finnish heritage as well, which may have been part of it. She was a little shorter than me and athletic, with wavy blondish hair and bluish green eyes. She was kind, sweet, innocent, and she occupied my heart and thoughts for a few years after we met.

I think my mother saw in her an opportunity for something 'worldly' to enter my life. Something that wouldn't parallel the teachings of the strict cult I was in. She knew that deep down in my heart, I was beyond their total control, and Christine was a way for me to experience life outside the cult. This could be a way to try and pull me out of it.

It didn't work like she may have anticipated, but it did begin to have a profound effect on how I coupled my personal desires with the practices of the cult. My ability to keep secrets evolved, and I became really good at it. In the end I was able to keep secrets from just about anyone, and boy could I lie. I was a great liar – so good, sometimes I myself had a hard time believing the things I could get away with.

HEALTH SUPPLEMENTS AND CLEANSES

Along with the essential oils and food storage, we were also instructed to do holistic cleanses. These were to purify our bodies of toxins we picked up when we were out in the world. We had our strict food laws, but that didn't mean we were protected from impurities acquired back when we used to eat anything. So we needed to cleanse ourselves, and from early on I remember cleanse after cleanse being preached from the pulpit.

Every day, we were instructed to take supplements, purchased through the house of Yahweh just like the essential oils and food for storage. We would take 1000 mg of vitamin C, two vitamin B tablets, a calcium tablet, cod-liver oil, flaxseed oil, and a couple more. Every morning we would take these, and we were made to feel like we were sinning if we failed to do so. My father just bought into it. He didn't question any of our instruction, ever. He had complete faith in everything he was told to do, and he did until the end.

Cherry flavored cod-liver oil? It was a little daffy. My favorite was the Colon Cleanse by Doctor Schultz. This one stuck in everyone's mind, and here's how it went: for one week, we'd take an eye-dropper full of this liquid that was basically habanero and cayenne extract in a shot of juice, twice a day. It was like fire-water, literally. Extremely picante and later that day, or else the next, the burn was felt again on the other end. So that was the first half of the cleanse;

the next week, we had to drink a mixture of some kind of clay that would expand inside the intestines and basically scrub out any matter that was stuck there.

We were given a booklet with the cleanse, and in the booklet was a picture of a bathtub with a 4-foot turd extending from the drain to the other end. Apparently, this had been lodged in some random guy's colon, and after the cleanse, he was purged of all that crap.

It's safe to say that there wasn't much scientific evidence behind any of what the House of Yahweh told its followers to do. Of course they wouldn't admit that, but there truly wasn't. All Yisrayl had to do was say that there was 'science behind it', and everyone else would agree. My father through his life continued to read books encouraged by the House of Yahweh – books on medicine written in the 1920s. But because of 'how evil the world is' (meaning conspiracies), the medical insight found in those books had been neglected by modern science.

Our beliefs shape our reality to some degree, but rocks when illogically stacked will eventually fall, as they did in the House of Yahweh. The truth is, people still got sick, still died from cancer; no one was immune from the natural stones of life that are thrown at us from time to time. According to the HoY, if we became sick, it was because we were sinning somehow. That's what we were told. How could it be anything else? We had all the teachings, and the proper food and supplements, so if we got sick, then sin must be the culprit, right?

I remember Bill Hawkins saying over the pulpit, "We've

had someone in the House cured of AIDS!" He said it enthusiastically, prompting a roar of cheers from the congregation.

MOVING TO THE FARM

My father was friends with a guy who was somewhat interested in the House of Yahweh, the guy he bought the food storage trailer from. He was a little better off than we were, financially, a nice guy with a good work ethic, just like my father. His name was Burt. He owned a good amount of real estate, and one of his properties was available for rent: a farmhouse on 40 acres of wooded land, near the newly built Aspen Ridge Middle School.

The house was old and very basic. It had a wood stove in the living room, used to heat the entire house during winter. It was a nice old farm, with three barn areas where we would eventually raise chickens, keep a couple of dogs and several cats, and store cords upon cords of firewood. Apple trees were scattered through a few acres of open field, and there was a cherry tree near the house. The only neighbor in walking distance from the farmhouse was the newly built Aspen Ridge school.

The summer before sixth grade I spent riding my skateboard around this area. The new school had freshly paved blacktop and plenty of space to skateboard. There really wasn't much else to do. No other kids were close by, although one day, a couple of girls called Karla and Greta said 'hi' to me while I was skateboarding. I couldn't tell why at the time, but I sensed I had something in common with them. They were sweet girls.

The older I got, the further I progressed through school, and the more it became clear to me that I was different from everyone else. Different in a way that I didn't necessarily want to be, but because of how my parents were raising me, I saw life through completely different lenses than everyone else. The problem was these lenses were calibrated to magical thinking, very far from logic.

Music became prohibited in the cult at this time – all forms of music were demonized. Yisrayl/Bill said we had a lot of sin in our lives, and we needed to repent and let go of it before we could have music again. So there were no more songs at Sabbath services, no classical music or anything like that. All of a sudden it was a "no-no" and that was that.

I remember some Saturdays, shortly after services when everyone else was resting, I would hide in my room listening to music with my headphones on. Everything from Beethoven's symphonies to the Beastie Boys, to Michael Jackson to Wu Tang. I had to keep my door locked in case someone knocked. I'd be chastised if I were caught listening to the music, especially on the Sabbath. They couldn't stop me from playing the piano, though, and my father never truly wanted me to stop. Still, he would question my motives for playing, and I'd spit out any response that would allow me to keep on playing. The truth is, I know that he let me win these arguments, and I know that he enjoyed the music I was trying to play.

THE MIKVAH

Every Friday we needed to prepare for the Sabbath. Since no work, no cooking, no personal pleasure could be done on the Sabbath, everything needed to be ready beforehand, to allow for a comfortable Saturday. All the meals for the next day needed to be cooked, and the house needed to be cleaned, to be considered holy. All this had to be finished before sunset, and during the winter, when the sun set early in the day, this was sometimes a challenge.

Right before Sabbath was often when family feuds would erupt. There was a lot of stress on everyone, and especially on Linda, my stepmother. She was basically responsible for the cooking, the cleaning, making sure that the clothes and bedding were washed… so of course if anything were to bother her, she'd let people know. Many Sabbaths, we would bicker right up to dinner, and sometimes it was difficult to start eating because of all that fighting. I can still remember my father sitting back in his chair with a disgusted look on his face, looking up and to the left, shaking his head, then leaning over to take his first bite of food. Sometimes I found this funny, because it diminished whatever anger was there.

On top of making sure everything was ready for the Sabbath, we needed to bathe and do what they call a Mikvah, or ablution, which is a tradition in Judaism. We would bathe, and then fill the tub with water and completely submerge ourselves. You might think it's difficult for a full grown man to fully submerge himself in a small tub without making a mess, and that is most definitely the truth. So what we'd do was roll around in the tub to make sure the water touched every part of our bodies.

This process of taking a Mikvah was even more bizarre when we went to Texas for the feasts. At home, my father would dunk first, then me, and then my stepmother. This was more or less the chain of command, since women were considered to be 'less clean' than men. In Texas, we had what most would consider public showers and restrooms. There was a much larger tub, really a water trough like horses use to drink from. The cringing side of this process was that we had to share it with several, if not hundreds, of other people. Sometimes the water got to looking a bit gross. Keep in mind that we were greatly discouraged from using public swimming pools.

The Mikvah happened every Friday. We'd work or go to school, clean, prepare food, wash up, and take the Mikvah. Then we were considered in a holy state, allowing us to be closer to Yahweh for the Sabbath. One thing I looked forward to was the good food. Linda cooked really well, despite how she and I could argue.

MIDDLE SCHOOL

Around the time of middle school it became obvious that I was different from everyone else, by which I mean it started to become more apparent to my peers. I already knew I was different, that my family was weird compared to everyone else's. Sometimes I tried to hide it, sometimes I took an attitude where I didn't care. I guess you could say I was luke-warm on the subject, 'lagom' in Swedish.

I was a misfit, to a great degree. My mother had taught me how to be a smart-ass, and the family dynamic at home didn't pair well with that skill. I was also a smart-ass at school, one of the deviants. I could succeed at something if I wanted to, but my efforts usually came in waves. Sometimes I would try, and do well. Sometimes I half-assed things, and didn't do well. I was a little above average in most of what I put my mind to, and so were my friends. And that's probably one of the reasons my friends and I didn't always try very hard.

I think my deviance arose from the extreme prohibition around various behaviors. Like when you tell a young child, "Don't do that", or "You'd better not do that." Without an explicit reason, the child will naturally want to do precisely that. The story about Playboy magazine mentioned earlier didn't put an end to pornography in my childhood, thanks to the cut-and-dried instructions against that and against fornication. I was told it was evil and wrong, and that was the end of it.

As an adult, I can clearly see the pointlessness of both

activities. Of course I love women, but an adult has the capacity to sense the rather materialistic side of these behaviors. On one end, I had a mother who was more relaxed about the idea of me looking at pictures of naked women, and on the other end, the House of Yahweh simply said, "No, it's evil, it's sinful, it will lead to eternal death" (although if you repent, you can be forgiven). It's sort of like what I said earlier about alcohol. Getting a taste of it here and there under mature guidance will likely provide a better cognitive approach to the subject. So my mother had the right idea. She knew there wasn't any harm, and she most likely knew there was more harm in trying to suppress normal boyish curiosities.

I never quit looking at pornography, but I found different ways to hide it. The material became more extreme, and therefore more hidden. Ultimately, I don't view the suppression as healthy, and I think it began to tie 'knots' in me that took a long time to untie, and then to move past.

I was deviant in my behavior in terms of pornography and also in my interactions with girls (although that was only deviant from the House of Yahweh perspective). I liked girls – who could blame me – and the fact that I was heavily instructed against pursuing any form of contact with them only drove me (subconsciously) to do just the opposite.

So I tried to get girlfriends, here and there, and I did get some, like Christine in Milwaukee. These were all puppy love scenarios and honestly innocent. The only problem was that my desire to be with these girls was driven by a deeper desire to simply be loved, held, and accepted, which I didn't truly feel until later in life. That need was certainly shaped by my relationship with my mother, and the view that I had of her interactions with men. More knots that I'd need to figure out how to untie, later in life.

As a side note, I see these sort of experiences in life are a blessing. From the standpoint of turning poison into medicine, when we're handed such a poison, the medicine we can make can be healing, not only for ourselves, but for all those who we might be able to help, when given the opportunity. Acceptance and honesty paired with compassion can truly empower any individual in a circumstance like that.

Of course I had to hide my deviance from my family. Any behavior that wasn't conducive to the teachings of the House of Yahweh surely needed to be kept secret from my father and stepmother. At the same time, any form of deviance that wouldn't be accepted by general society would have to be kept hidden from just about everyone, except of course my friends, who might even give a sort of praise or show acceptance.

The pre-teen to early-teen period can be difficult for any child. If my behaviors were so very different from the normal "realm of deviance", then I wouldn't have received acceptance from other kids who also came from difficult households.

In that light, you could say that my unusual family dynamic had a role in shaping who I made friends with.

The so-called 'popular' kids in school shunned me from their social circles. I was weird in many ways, so I could overlook a lot of girls avoiding me, but when the popular kids don't let you into their group, there's only so many other groups you can turn to, like what the popular kids referred to as the 'scrubs'. These were kids who didn't have much money in their families, at least not apparently. They didn't wear the popular clothes, didn't have new things like the popular kids did. Then there were the 'geeks' who didn't care about those things. They did well in school for the most part, but they didn't hang out with anyone else. I guess you could say I drifted between all the groups and made a few friends in each. When the majority of one group didn't want me in their network, I moved on to one that would.

THE MOVE TO ISHPEMING

I didn't really live in a neighborhood for the sixth and seventh grades. The farm house was a couple miles or more from other houses (or at least houses with another child my age). So the neighborhood drama didn't start until I moved from the farm house to the first house my father bought, in Ishpeming, near a bluff called Jasper Knob.

This home was a 20-minute walk from Ishpeming High School and a 40-minute walk from the local middle school, Phelps, where I started elementary school. That's the neighborhood where the drama would soon begin with me and another 'local deviant'.

Around the seventh grade, I started feeling deeply unaccepted by my peers. I didn't know how to show myself, had no clue who I was or how to interact with others. The response I got from many kids at school was simply that they hated me. That sounds harsh, but it's how kids can be, and I'm certainly not the only one who dealt with it.

I'm not sure what the exact reasons were, but we decided to buy a house. I think the owner of the farm house needed to let his mother move in, or he wanted to sell it. Either way, we had to move. My father looked at a couple houses in Ishpeming: a large duplex for $19,000, and a large house near Jasper Bluff for $27,000. We looked at both, and my father contemplated buying the cheaper one, but my stepmother and I both loved the expensive house, which had a two-car garage, a small backyard, two kitchens, a dining room, five bedrooms, and a full-size attic.

I even told my father I'd give up my allowance to move into this house, and that was what happened.

The truth of the matter is I did honestly like the house, but the bigger issue was that I'd have the chance to go to a different school, where the kids didn't hate me so. At least not yet. When we were preparing to move out of the farm house, we had two dogs – two blue-heelers that we'd got from a breeder in Texas, a member of the House of Yahweh. These were like any dogs, playful and fun to be around, although when they humped each other my father would kick them pretty hard. They were both male dogs, so that was sinful behavior, according to us.

Owning animals in the House of Yahweh was a clear-cut thing. According to the Bible, man has domain over all living things, so in a certain light, it's as if non-human life were irrelevant. As we prepared to move, my father noted that we wouldn't be able to take the dogs, so we'd have to 'put them down'. He drove a bulldozer to the northern edge of our property and dug a large hole. My stepmother and I were standing outside the front door of the house watching each other when we heard a loud bang. Linda was looking down at her feet as she flinched. Tears were pouring down her face. Bang, the second shot went off and her crying intensified. I'll never forget those tears of hers that day. It was a rare moment when she let her true feelings show.

3. EARLY TEEN LOW

My childhood at that point hit an all-time low. I did things that I became ashamed of later in life. Thankfully, probably through guidance from my father, I was able to get past a lot of it, and had I not, I probably would've ended up in jail.

My deviance grew tremendously after we moved to Ishpeming. I hooked up with some of the local 'bad kids' in the neighborhood, and the next thing I knew, I was taking part in vandalism and breaking into cars. The idea of getting free stuff wasn't my motivation, but simply the high I got from doing it. That excitement allowed me to completely escape all other aspects of my reality.

It was then that I tried smoking marijuana for the first time. One of the local kids had a little, with a small pipe. He took the first hit and then handed the pipe to me. He held the lighter. I inhaled deeply and then coughed like I'd never coughed before. I seriously thought I was going to throw up. I couldn't take it, and I said I needed to go home.

That happened over the span of about three minutes. I hopped on my bike and started down the hill for my 12-second ride home. I don't remember much after that, except playing on the living room floor and acting goofy in front of my stepmother. She was laughing hysterically at me. "What's gotten into you?" I was most undoubtedly high, but I didn't know it, and neither did she. It was pretty funny, though.

My behavior changed around the eighth grade, and I

became much more resistant to all forms of authority. As the new kid at Phelps Middle School, the other students found my rebellious behavior funny at first. So I gave into it. As they got tired of, or used to, my random acts of outburst, or my picking on other not-so-popular kids, I would just try harder. Eventually I put myself back in a similar situation to my previous school: once again, my peers didn't like me.

At all.

The faculty didn't like me either. Although my behavior was sometimes witty, my smart-ass-ness could drive them nuts – so nuts, they'd try pretty hard to put me into difficult situations.

For example, there was a time in band class when a window got broken. A student had tipped a chair into it. I didn't see it happen, but I saw the broken glass, so I went over to help pick it up. I looked at the window and saw a piece of glass sticking out from the edge, and I said to another student, should I punch that piece out? He responded with excitement, "I dare you."

So I did, without hesitation. I didn't really think much of it, since I had punched out windows before, without a problem. Well this time was the charm, and I ended up with quite a wound.

I went downstairs to the nurse's office, and she told me that I needed stitches, that I should go wait upstairs for my father to pick me up. When I got upstairs, the principal came over and told me I was suspended, for breaking a window. I was in shock – I couldn't believe it, because I hadn't broken the window. I told her so, and she said, "I don't want to hear it. You're suspended for breaking school property."

I was pissed. So I went with her to the band teacher's office, and he explained to her how the window had been broken. The excitement was too much for me, and I was embarrassed to cry in front of other students. Later, I would deny that ever happened.

So I got stitches, and I had to wear a weird apparatus that allowed my tendon to heal properly, because I'd cut the tendon in my middle finger, above my knuckle. I still remember the nurse being a complete idiot, with his hemostats underneath my slightly severed tendon, pulling it up about half-an-inch or so above my knuckle. "The tendon is cut and it could break" the nurse said. My father told me in the truck on the way to the specialist's office that he'd almost knocked the nurse out for doing that.

It was a little traumatic. Not the stitches, not the principal, not even seeing my tendon in my hand, but the idea that I might not be able to play the piano anymore. Thankfully, I can. Thankfully, I have here on my finger a reminder of how wounds heal, and of who I was, and of who I am now.

SOMETHING STARTS TO CHANGE

My father caught me in a deviant moment, where he somehow just knew I was guilty. Despite my professional lies – the way I was able to convince anyone (except maybe him) – he persisted with how I needed to be honest, how I needed to tell the truth.

He told me story after story, analogy after analogy. He knew I was guilty, and he also knew he would forgive me. But what he knew most, is that (if only for myself) I needed to be honest. So I confessed. I told him that I had done it. I had robbed the place.

He drove me back to the police station. The police were in awe. They even told me that they had believed my story, and that I was very lucky they didn't put me in juvenile detention. Instead, the owner of the establishment that I had violated settled things with my father. I had to write a letter of apology so that everyone in the venue could see it. And yes, I was ashamed, very ashamed, but not as ashamed as I was lost, and in need of escape.

Had everyone there known that part of the story, they might not have been so offended by my behavior. But it was more or less the last straw, not for my father, but for me. My father would of course take me to the elders, and they would tell me what I needed to do, but he didn't scream at me, he didn't hurt me. He didn't even try to make me think that he would do those things. He knew that I knew it was the last straw, because I had 'fessed-up.

That was the beginning of the end of my deviant

behavior. With the help of my father, I was able to move past it. How it all worked out so well, I'm not sure, but I think maybe it's because my father had a special kind of compassion for me.

By the end of the eighth grade, I was spending a lot of time by myself. I had some friends here and there who I'd hang out with, but for the most part, I was alone. It really couldn't be any other way. It was as weird for me as for the other students that I left school three times a year to go to Texas for a week or two. By then, I was used to the other students asking, "Why don't you just move to Texas?" Like it was my choice.

The snow was melting, and summer was around the corner. I knew most of it would be spent working, whether with my father, doing landscaping, or working my second year at the Milwaukee Summerfest.

The motto in the House of Yahweh was, "hurry hurry hurry, work work work." The more we worked, the more money we'd be able to give to "Yahweh's work". My father preferred that I work with him, but I insisted that I wanted to return to Summerfest again.

The summer between the seventh and eighth grades, my mother was dating the head of security for the Summerfest grounds. He was a nice guy, sort of a jock, family-guy type. When he and my mother took me and my cousin Whitney there, the first thing I did was to look for a job. I don't remember the motivation, but I was determined to find a place to work. I was 13 at the time.

I went from vendor to vendor to see if they needed

someone to work for them. Eventually, I found a booth run by people from India. The owner of the shop was named Wazir.

I spent three summers working for Wazir. He paid me $5 an hour. It was worth it at the time, because it allowed me to check out the fairgrounds everyday, and to party with the other kids at night. I was even able to smuggle alcohol into the grounds, to ensure excitement after dark, but that didn't happen much until my last year at Summerfest, when I was 15.

CONFESSION

Although some aspects of my behavior were changing, others weren't, and I would continue to deviate from the religious instructions given to me by the House of Yahweh. Without a doubt, my father (so distant in some regards) was still able to reach me and help cure certain deviant traits in my behavior. I quit certain behaviors, especially those that involved misfortune to others. As far as girls were concerned, that was a habit that the House of Yahweh would have difficulty breaking.

I was around the age of 14, not much older or younger. The House of Yahweh imposed a ban on music from our personal lives, as well as during the religious services. This ban on music had been happening for a couple years at that point. As Yisrayl had said, the ban was due to sin on our part, and thanks to new understanding of a prophecy done by Yisrayl, we would have to make confession from then on. That would bring us all closer to Yahweh, and confer more holiness.

Confession in the House of Yahweh was similar to confession in the Catholic church, except instead of confessing through a perforated wall to a priest who's facing away from you, we had to sit down at a table face-to-face with two elders, who would scold us for our transgressions. As long as we appeared to be sorry, they would forgive us.

This point in time was a little odd, and maybe the first real quake before the big rumble of fundamentalism really roared in. We had all been baptized, but now that didn't count. We all had our ears pierced with an awl on the doorpost of Yisrayl's office, but that didn't count either. All those things needed to be done again after our first confession, in order for them to truly count.

The first confession took place at the end of the feast of Passover, for those who didn't live in Abilene, Texas. Those who did live there were first on the list. This "teaching" came over the pulpit during the middle of the feast, to prepare people for what they would have to go through.

When I first started to write this book, I left out my personal experience with confession, because I was embarrassed and ashamed of what others might think of me. A part of my ego got the best of me. However, I now see that what happened is pertinent to this story, and it might also function as a beacon to some readers out there. In the end, what I confessed to was agonizingly difficult for a 14-year-old boy – it was the most difficult thing I'd had to do in my life, by far.

To provide some context, I should give a background as to what led to the confessional table. When I was around the age of puberty, I became very curious with exploring my body. A friend of mine also had this same curiosity. On various occasions, he and I spent a few hours together alone, where we would touch each other. Admittedly, there was excitement. We would talk and fantasize about girls that we liked. We'd make jokes, laugh, and enjoy the stimulation of each other's hands on our genitals. These events led to what was ultimately intercourse. It happened one brief time, for no longer than about five seconds. That was when I realized that what we were doing wasn't for me. I was maybe 12 years old, and a light went off in my head. That was that. We stopped, never tried it again, and maintained our friendship.

I didn't really think of it afterward. I didn't feel ashamed, although I knew that what I had done was against the cult rules. However, when time for confession came, I started to tremble with fear.

I sat in front of the elders. I confessed to stealing, smoking, drinking, slander, lying, looking at pornography, what have you. But, when I spoke of this last sin, the two elders looked at me with great concern. Elder John Bragg from Maine said, "To forgive you of this sin, you need to tell your father what you did". I couldn't hold back the tears. I begged to not have to do that. It just seemed so wrong for him to be the person I told, but so it went.

I had no idea how I was going to tell him, or whether there was a way I could lie my way out. But there wasn't. We were walking together on the compound, about a stone's throw from his bus-house. I can still clearly remember looking at the hard red clay ground under my feet, watching my tears moisten it ever so slightly.

"Just tell me what it was so we can get through this," my father said.

"I can't," shaking my head.

"Just tell me."

Choking on my words, with tears pouring down my face, I said, "I laid down with another man. I didn't like it afterwards. I didn't want to do it again."

He approached me with calmness in his voice and his eyes. He put his hand on my shoulder and said it was okay.

"I did that too when I was a boy," he said.

I thought to myself, "I don't want to know that, and I still didn't want to have to tell you this."

"Brandon, there were boys in my town that would have sex with animals," he said, becoming very relaxed about the situation.

We headed back to the sanctuary where I had made the confession so he could explain to the elders that I had told him what I'd done. Both elders looked at me, and elder John said, "Now don't you feel better after this?"

"No," I replied looking him dead in the eye.

It's taken me a long time to not look back on this with some sense of shame or embarrassment. I never even talked out loud about that situation until I started writing this book. First, I told the story in confidence to two close friends, and as time went on, I spoke about it a bit more. The only shame in this part of my story was being falsely convinced that a child has no right to feel such innocent and natural curiosity, and to eventually decide what's right for him.

Once confession was over, there were a few more ceremonies lined up. After services one day, my friend Jake and I were joking around, talking about the re-baptism and ear-awling. We thought it would be funny to convince my father that along with all these "re-dos", we would all have to be re-circumcised as well. So we went up to my father with serious looks on our faces, and expressions of discontent. I told him that we had to get re-circumcised. His jaw dropped, his eyes opened wide, and he said, "Nooooo" (with emotion extending through the 'o').

I said, "Yeah Dad, what are we going to do?"

"I don't know," he responded.

Then Jake started laughing, and I couldn't hold back either. "We're just kidding, dad."

Relief washed over his face. "I'm not sure they could take any more off," he said.

A side note about the circumcision. It wasn't that big of a deal for me, since I was already circumcised, but for many men, it was quite a hassle to deal with.

You can only imagine, having a much larger piece of flesh removed from your penis as an adult would require a bit more time to heal. The stories were horrendous. First, the congregation was convinced that an uncircumcised penis was unclean and could carry a lot of bacteria, which is mainly why it needed to be done. Then they would set up a make-shift medical center inside of an old trailer home, where a couple of elders would do the procedure with razor blades and some local anesthetic. There was even an older man, most likely in his mid-60s, who circumcised himself. Shortly after this was done, people would complain about their stitches, difficulty urinating, and the extreme pain of waking up with an erection.

Again, consider the absurdity of a fully grown man being told that he will not make it into the kingdom of heaven because he isn't circumcised.

A SUMMER OF SINS

The summer between my freshman and sophomore years of high school may have been the roughest of my childhood. I had a lot of 'fun', so to speak, and I had a lot of steam to let off, from my first year of high school.

I had wanted to go back to my old school, even though I was told by many there that they still hated me. But because I'd been suspended in the eighth grade, the superintendent for Westwood High told me I needed one more year at Ishpeming High to prove myself. The year didn't go that bad, the upper-classmen really didn't bother with us freshman. Of course I was a little weird, the way I behaved sometimes, and then there was that 'religious thing' that I never really talked about in detail. The other kids wouldn't have really got it, anyway.

So I didn't get picked on much more than was usual, although once I was approached by someone who wanted to fight. I had no idea of the reason; there really wasn't one. This kid just wanted to fight me. He was an upper-classman, and we were in the same math class, and one day, he said he wanted to fight me. I knew I wouldn't do it. My father would've been very angry at me if I did, and if he ever found out that I actually fought, it would mean more counselling from the elders. Taking a few blows would at least be something new.

So this guy Dan said "after school by the gully", and I had to show up, otherwise I'd be a coward. I didn't really know what would happen, and I didn't know how much it would hurt. I remembered getting beaten up in Texas once, and that really hurt, those kids knew how to hit hard. At least now I knew how to tighten my stomach and take a hit. But I didn't think it would be all that bad.

All the other kids, 20 or so, showed up to the fight and made a big circle in the snow. I told most of my friends that I wasn't going to fight back. I told Dan that I wouldn't fight, and the truth is, I didn't want to. He pushed me a couple times, then brought me to the ground with a wrestling move. I let it happen. He punched me in the ear, but I didn't really feel it. It was winter.

We rolled in the snow a bit, and I wasn't resisting. "Fight!" he yelled.

"I'm not going to fight you." I laid there tucked in the snow, to block his fists from my face. I let him hit me everywhere else, so my father wouldn't know. He punched me a few more times, then got up and left.

The other kids seemed disappointed, and probably they wanted to see more action. I moaned a little to make it look bad, but it wasn't. Within 40 minutes I was able to get back home and pretend like nothing had happened. I don't think my father ever knew what had happened that day.

One of my friends told me it was probably best that I hadn't fought back, just because it made Dan look like an asshole. And he was one – there was never a reason for that fight. But there might have been a reason why I felt like I needed to be beaten. When you grow up under a religion like I did, you always feel guilty about something.

Then the summer came. The school year was over, and

I was going to work at Summerfest again, but this time as a 15-year-old. I had it in the back of my mind that I'd eventually have to confess to whatever I did, so I tried to figure ways to downplay the inevitable confession before I committed the 'sin'. I suppose that was silly of me. Fornication is fornication, and smoking pot is also what it is. But I'd had kind of a shitty year, and steam to let out.

At the Summerfest grounds, there was this club area called Club Kiss, where all the kids would get together and dance. That never happened in my hometown, and I did like to dance. I've always liked to dance. But hey – now there's girls, a lot of them! Tall ones, short ones, blondes and Hispanics, and it felt good to get attention. Even some of the older guys who were in their 20s were nice to me, and brought me into their circles.

I looked a lot older than I was. I told everyone I was 18, so when they saw me carrying my own flask full of 'Everclear', they didn't think twice about offering to buy me beer, or to pass the joint my way. Needless to say, a couple of nights I became heavily intoxicated.

And then I met this girl, named Jenny.

She liked to dance and flirt. Blonde, voluptuous, a couple tattoos, and 19. She also thought I was 18. We had met up a couple times at Club Kiss to dance and make out. She gave me her phone number, so I could meet up with her and her friends, and a couple nights we did. The first night was more bizarre. Losing one's virginity must always be strange, for anyone. The first half was normal, and even romantic, on the shore of Lake Michigan under the stars.

Even the stink of rotting fish was absent that night. During the second half, Jenny's friend and younger sister (still older than me) and two random African American guys from Kansas were watching us from a distance. I remember thinking that the experience was about as mediocre as it possibly could be. I even up-played the climax so I wouldn't seem so bored. But really it was my first time, and I'm sure it must have looked silly.

I tried not to think about the potential repercussions of this experience. It caused too much cognitive dissonance, and the last thing I wanted to think about while still in Milwaukee was the wrath I'd get from the elders after I confessed to this stuff. A few days after, Jenny and I met up again to fool around in a park. I figured, "What difference does it make if I do it twice?" At least the second time wasn't quite so mediocre.

I was used to feeling alone, in most of my experiences. I couldn't talk to my father about certain things, for obvious reasons, and if I'd mentioned the fight to my mother, she might've talked to my dad about it. She had told my father about Christine, which caused me to hold back from talking to her about other things.

But I did ask her, "Mom, what would you say if I had sex with Jenny?"

"I would sue her for statutory rape. You didn't sleep with her, did you?"

"No, of course not."

"I thought so. Don't even try to make me think that you did." She said.

101

Jenny had left a disgusting hickey on my neck. "What's your father going to think of that?" asked my mother, laughing. I felt a bit paranoid, since I didn't know how to hide it. I knew it wouldn't go away in just a couple of days, so I needed to do something.

So I took a cigar, a big Churchill-size one, got it burning good, took a shot of 'everclear', and burned the hickey. At least that way, I could make up another story.

When I went home to my father, he looked at my neck and said, "What's that?"

I responded with intensity, lying about how a guy at Summerfest poked my neck with a cigar. I'm not sure he believed me, but he was at least gullible enough to not take it further. My father was pretty gullible, and I often had to use that to my advantage.

BACK TO SCHOOL

School time came around, and I was a bit relieved that I'd be back with kids who I'd already spent part of my childhood with. I knew I needed to behave differently this time around.

I couldn't be cocky, I couldn't try to stand out. Because I tended to be that way that naturally,

I needed to hold back as much as I could. just so they'd give me another chance. Which they did.

Shortly after school started, the feast of Tabernacles was already approaching. I'd be leaving for Texas, and I'd have to make up all my homework while gone. But I never really did – I just let my grades suffer. The elders would tell me, "Just pass, they're not teaching you Yahweh's Laws, they're disciples of Satan. Tribulation will be here before you graduate from high school anyway."

I even considered dropping out of school, since that was what a lot of other kids in the House of Yahweh did; but it would've caused complications between my mother and father, and maybe the local community and my father as well. So the elders didn't really see it as a viable option, just yet.

We were making more preparations for the "Time of Tribulation". Everyone was investing in gas masks, charcoal-impregnated chemical suits, water purifiers. We were some of the first doomsday preppers, like what you see on TV today, but minus the heavy fire-power (thankfully.)

This paranoia often brought out goofy behavior.

I remember standing outside my camper talking with Jake. It was about 80 degrees outside, in the dry Texas heat, and here came my father in the distance. He always walked with a bounce, so I could tell it was him. But this time, he was walking toward the camper in a bright yellow rain-suit. I'm thinking, "What the fuck?" He had a gas mask hanging around his neck like re-enacting a scene from 'Back to the Future'.

"Here's your gas mask." He handed me an olive-drab canvas-back.

"What the hell are you doing?" I asked, as Jake held back his laughter.

"Contrails, Brandon. Some planes just flew over, and they left their contrails. Just be prepared," he told me.

But I had much bigger things on my mind. How was I going to tell my counselor that I had fornicated over the summer? I told it to the elders during confession, and they told me that I needed to talk to my counselor about it before I could be forgiven.

The Day of Atonement was coming up, too – every year, there was a day where we wouldn't eat or drink anything for 24 hours. It was a practice of fasting, supposed to bring us closer to Yahweh and holiness.

I'd been planning to talk to my counselor, Jeff, that day. He was so sheltered from anything but the House of Yahweh, I'm not sure he knew much about the subject. So I went in and told him. I told him that I'd had sex with a girl, twice. And boy, did he lay into me. He asked me if she was on birth control – I said I didn't know. He asked me if I wore a condom – I said I did. Then he proceeded to tell me that she might still be pregnant, and that I might have a lot of diseases from what I had done. I had long been scared and paranoid about STDs, but much more so after that. He told me that I needed to fast to be forgiven, for at least two days.

I cried in front of him, said I was sorry, but he showed no empathy. He told me I needed to pray, and that I'd also need to do cleanses to purify my body of sexual diseases. "Yisrayl Hawkins says that no matter what, if you fornicate, you will get diseases. You have diseases now, and you need to cleanse yourself, and start by fasting."

There was a side of me that wanted to call bullshit. When he told me she might still be pregnant, my first thought was, "Yeah, right." But if I didn't believe in the House of Yahweh, at least a little, I wouldn't have been confessing in the first place. Had I known the real truth about Jeff and his scandals with women in the House of Yahweh, I wouldn't have listened to anything he had to say. At least other elders would have admitted that they'd done the same thing.

In the end, didn't eat or drink water for two days. I let the feeling of guilt take the place of my hunger. Shortly after that, I was back in Michigan and back in school. I was taking two math classes at that time. I wanted to take what was called 'fifth-year math' in high school, and to do that, I needed to double up on Algebra 2 and Geometry. My teacher for both of those back-to-back classes was named Mr. Wigg. He was a hard-ass to me, which was one of the

105

biggest reasons why I liked him. When I got back to his class after that feast, he asked me about what I'd been doing down there, and I told him a bit about it. His eyes opened, and I saw a great amount of empathy that I'd never forget. He knew, and soon all the teachers would know. From then on, they all 'had my back' in such a subtle way, I wasn't even aware of it until after high school.

CULT DRAMA

A lot happened in the House of Yahweh around that time. A sect had broken off and tried to take a bunch of followers with it. They even set up a camp not far from the one in Clyde, during a feast. It was shortly after we'd started practicing confession.

Some elders had gotten together and written a letter. I was never able to read it, or even to hear it read, but I heard about it, since rumors ran rampant through the House of Yahweh. Elders from Wisconsin seemed to be behind it, and families were torn apart because of it. It was quite the dramatic scenario.

From my understanding, it all had something to do with how Yisrayl Hawkins had conducted the confessions, and how it was just him and two elders who were running everything in the cult. These were just rumors, coming from the other side – the people who had formed a sect.

The rumors on the House of Yahweh side were much more entertaining. They said these people were contacting spirits, becoming mediums, and having conversations with the dead. They had come up with their own interpretation of the Bible and were ultimately being ruled by Satan. Obviously, anything that went against the House of Yahweh's teachings was Satanic, according to their standards.

Looking back, I wonder what these elders really knew about Yisrayl, and why they really chose to do what they did. There was no violence, so far as I know. Just petty drama, if anything. Shortly after the sect broke off, they dissolved as a group (or so I heard), and I don't recall any of them re-joining the House of Yahweh.

This event was most likely the biggest thing that happened within the cult. A lot of spooky stories and rumors were circulating, about how people were talking to demons. It might be true that, in all forms of extreme fundamentalist religions like those, people become convinced that they can talk to spirits. I remember when I was a child seeing a man who seemed to be having some kind of episode. Not epilepsy – not so extreme as that. It happened in the middle of services at the feast. Two elders came right away, picked him up out of his chair, and carried him away.

Rumors circulated from that, as well. He was said to have been speaking in tongues after getting possessed by demons, which is why the elders took him away, to pray over him. Looking back, it was theatrical, but in the moment, it was unusual and uncomfortable.

Rumors were always buzzing in the House of Yahweh, about anything and everything. But when you think about it, what else was there to do?

Abiding by all those laws was impossible anyway, mainly because they were always changing, and open to interpretation.

I remember some rumors that spread about myself and a girl I had been "talking to" in the House of Yahweh. Her name was Karen. She was a little older than me, and very pretty. We liked each other, enjoyed each other's company.

We'd spoken to each other before the rules changed, which happened very soon after. Every feast, there would be a new story about her, about us, about what people thought we were doing. One day, my father and an elder came up to me and told me that she had fornicated at some point, and that I could never have her as a wife. I could have her as a maidservant, but not a wife – that is, if I ever wanted to be a priest.

Shortly after, I was told her family left the House of Yahweh and moved back to California. Years later I was told that they were manipulated financially, and had lost a lot of money due to the House of Yahweh.

THE BRIDE'S PRICE

When the rules on talking to women changed, so did the whole dynamic between men and women. Soon some men and just about all the women started wearing burkas, like some Muslim women wear. Then, in the sanctuary, there was a barrier running right down the center, separating the men from the women.

New teachings came out on how we were never to speak with women we weren't related to, or who weren't our wives. The only reason, ever, to speak to another woman, would be to pursue marriage with her. If you wanted to do that, and you were a young man, then you needed to talk to your father first, then to your counselors (who were elders). Then they would go to the girl's counselors (who were elders' wives), and then to her father, and then to the girl. Talk about anticipation of rejection. In reality, by that point, it was really hard to build up any interest in women at all.

If men were caught talking to girls in public, they would surely be spoken to about it by an elder. People were of course always willing to tell on other people in the House of Yahweh. It was a dog-eat-dog cult, in many regards. The buildings were restructured too, encouraging the separation between men and women. No longer would the opposite sex be seen eating together, and rarely would they be seen shopping in the same area. Wives and husbands would only be able to share time together behind the closed doors of their homes.

Then there was the idea of the bride's price, where men

110

had to pay the father of a girl whatever money he demanded for marrying his daughter. But that changed too, and instead of the father getting the money, we were instructed to pay the House of Yahweh directly. That basically meant paying Yisrayl, because he set the price. I believe the minimum amount was $15,000.

It seemed like a great deal for Yisrayl, especially if it came from someone working for the House of Yahweh. They probably didn't earn much more than $3/hour, and they'd most likely end up some kind of slave for the duration of their time in the cult. I'm sure they had to sign a lot of papers agreeing to that. But in reality, this would be a rare or non-existent problem, because most men, and especially young men, were left out of the circle.

The young girls who (one would think) might be pursued by those young men were in fact being pursued by elders who already had wives.

Although there was one exception, and a significant one for me. A girl named Samantha wanted to talk to me, when I was around 15. She was pretty and young, and it definitely took me by surprise, but I'll get back to that story later.

THEY CALLED IT YESHIVAH

We had a class for young men called "Yeshivah" that started around 2001-2002. It was considered a training program, to raise young men to be priests. This was a daily activity throughout all the feast times.

There was also more Bible studies, more work, more of what to do and what not to do. There was even a financial scam involved, beyond the free labor. Because we spent whole days in this Yeshivah class, and we needed to eat, we needed to buy food from them. We spent upwards of $18 dollars per meal, in advance, only to receive something smaller than what you might receive on a 3-hour flight. Some people were really pissed.

I remember another guy named Brandon, an elder's son who couldn't help but show his frustration. He was right, and justified – it was a total scam. I'll also never forget the day they salted the water. You see, everything we ate had to be salted, because the Bible says, "Salt every sacrifice." This had been a standard instruction for a few years. We had to salt everything, and we were only allowed to use a certain type of salt, sold by the House of Yahweh. 'Real Salt', it was called.

Maybe someday people will realize the connection between the brands being sold and how Bill Hawkins made investment profits outside his cult. Shortly after we were told to salt all of our food, someone asked Yisrayl (Bill) if we should salt our drinks, too, and he said, "Why not?"

Soon after that, people were putting excess amounts of

salt in everything, especially their water. One guy said to me one day, after I put a tiny dash of salt in my drink, "You know, Yisrayl will put a teaspoon of salt in his water." As if now it were law to use certain measurements of salt.

During Yeshivah, in the hot dry fields of Clyde, Texas, we had only one 5-gallon container of water for everyone to share, and there was so much salt in the water that it became undrinkable for most. Those of us who didn't want to drink salt water were more or less ostracized from the group at that time.

Yeshivah studies were a chore, but they were also a way to separate us from the rest of the followers, and to give us some sort of praise. Other boys who weren't in Yeshivah were often looked at as less serious about following Yahweh's laws.

I couldn't blame them for not wanting to be a part of it. It was utterly boring at times, and it consumed at least 12 hours of the day. I had no choice about being in it, and neither did anyone else really; then the kids who really wanted to be in it, were mostly left out. I only wonder how this fit into the structure of the whole scheme of things.

I look back on those days and recall the veracity of the elders, as they gazed at us boys with what I now see as false encouragement. For years, I wondered how many of those elders were fooled, but now seems more certain in my mind that most of them were in on the scheme. And why wouldn't they be, with such powers as to take multiple wives, and to have all others look up to you with praise?

WHAT'S IN A NAME?

A few years before this, when I was still about 12, the congregation were being encouraged to change their names. Everyone, most definitely, would change their last name to Hawkins. It was all a part of being "a part of the family".

Then Yisrayl would choose Hebrew names for all of us. Even my father had his name legally changed, to Yishayah Eben Salo Hawkins. At school one day, a teacher asked me about this name change. I had my name changed socially, but not legally, and I am thankful for that. The name I was referred to by my father and priests was Nehemyah, and my full Hebrew name was Nehemyah Neri Hawkins.

My father had originally chosen another name for me, but after speaking with Bill, he gave me that one. Bill Hawkins pretty much chose the names for everyone. At that point in the House of Yahweh, his behavior was shifting from that of a leader to that of a dictator.

"Nehemyah," an elder or another boy in Yeshivah would call me, or my father would call from downstairs. I have many memories of hearing this name. Maybe I never got it legally changed because it would have caused complications in public school, or maybe the elders were worried that my mother would contest it.

I do believe in the importance of a name, even one as random (or as last-minute) as mine seemed to be – at birth, my father wanted to name me Jalmer, but my mother wouldn't let him. In any case, being named Brandon Walter Salo has shaped my life, no doubt. I once met a lady in

Helsinki who thought Jalmer was a better name than Brandon; she was a rather Old School Finnish lady, I thought.

"Jalmer," she said, rolling the 'r' dramatically, "is a much better name than Brandon."

What's in a name? I was asked that question in English class when we read 'The Crucible'. Mr. Bradley had us answer that question, and maybe that's when the wheels of my subconscious really started turning. In the classes I had with Mr. Bradley, I was given many such questions to ponder, and I even started to like him – because I didn't at first.

And then one day, I got the idea that he'd make a great man in the House of Yahweh, so I decided to share some things about the religion with him. He looked at me with wide-open eyes, similar to those Mr. Wigg had given me when I returned from Texas.

He said, "Brandon, if this is what you believe in, then that's great, you need to do this, but I'm sorry, it's not for me."

I don't remember being very disappointed, but I do remember that being just about everything I needed to hear. In a way, that was the beginning to me being saved.

It was very weird having two names, like officially having two identities. I even had an ID card with the HoY name on it. I rarely showed it to anyone.

ABSENCE FROM HONESTY

In my mind, it always seemed that I was going back and forth with the House of Yahweh. I wanted to try, I wanted to believe, I wanted to keep the laws we were instructed to keep. But then my will would waver, especially in the case of pursuing girls outside of the cult.

I was lonely in so many ways, and desiring the attention of females was a huge weakness that stayed with me and kept morphing as my life went on. An anxiety I had from a young age involved hearing the phone ring. There were times when a girl looked up my number in the phone book and gave me a call. It was worse if it happened on a Saturday.

The girl would call, and I'd stand there in front of my father and stepmother while talking to her. It couldn't have been more awkward. After the conversation was over, I'd be questioned on what I was doing and why she had called. Most of the time I didn't even know why they called – they just wanted to talk. So from about the age of 12, every time the phone rang, a jolt of anxiety would shoot from my gut to my teeth. And as my teeth tingled, I'd clench my fists and hope it wasn't a girl who was calling.

I succumbed to the adolescent fantasies of love and romance at a very young age. The idea of falling in love was so exciting! I wanted to be in love. The week-long 'relationships' a child might have in middle school only teased those ideas. I fell in love too quickly, and got hurt too fast, but all of those times were still an escape from my

116

family. It was the only way I knew to deal with being so lonely. It was the only way I could escape, and so it was worth it, even though it was always short-lived.

As I got older and came to the end of puberty, my fascination with sex paralleled my longing for romance and a sustainable relationship. I still looked at pornography, as did my peers at school, but I also read a lot about sex. You could say it was one of the few things I actually studied. It seemed so fascinating. And because it was such a taboo, so far removed from the life that I was supposed to be living, my curiosity was driven through the roof. So in the end I wasn't able to hold back my desire to pursue girls at school, and eventually I experienced a relationship – the strongest I'd had to that point.

I liked a blonde girl, shorter than me, who I thought was really cute. One day, possibly the last day of my junior year, I was sitting on a brick ledge inside the school. She walked by while a friend was talking with me. I asked her for her number, and she gave it to me. That was the beginning of that 'one' relationship many of us had in high school.

At that point in time, I was also in the process of being betrothed (or engaged) to a girl in the House of Yahweh. That sounds extreme, and in some ways it was, because it was an arranged ordeal. But that circumstance also prevented any emotions from entering into the situation. It was like it wasn't real to me – and it wasn't – but it grew into a very difficult situation for a lot of people as time went on.

(SOMEWHAT) ARRANGED MARRIAGES

So this girl named Samantha (pseudonym) had pursued conversation with me. I was approached by my father one day, and he told me that she was interested in pursuing marriage, and that if I decided to speak with her, that would be an opportunity to get to know her. But on the other hand, if I didn't want to marry her, I didn't have to. I was 15 years old, and though it may sound extreme to be 'pursued for marriage' at that age, that was the only reason two single people of opposite sexes were allowed to communicate.

We spoke face to face during the feasts. Maybe two or three times per feast, and under the supervision of two elders and two elders' wives while we spoke across a table or corridor. The truth is, I don't remember much of those conversations, because there wasn't much to them. I'm sure we both were distracted by the authority figures hovering over us. I feel there was some sort of attraction. She was pretty, I think she had similar opinions of me, but all in all, we never had a chance of getting to know each other.

I had a romantic fantasy about her, thanks to this situation. Not 'romantic' in the typical sense, but in a sense that paralleled the dynamics of the cult. I'd think about what it might be like to actually be married to this girl – how I would go about doing it. How I'd get a job in Texas, and provide a dwelling space, and how we'd have children, and how we'd grow together in Yahweh's laws while we waited for the Times of Tribulation ahead.

And even though the images in my head felt romantic,

the way it would've likely played out could not be called the norm. Bear in mind the conditions at Clyde, Texas. It's sparse, and dusty, with the Mesquite trees widely separated by thorn plants and small patches of frail prairie grass. It was something that no one in their right mind would desire, especially when you think about your neighbors, constantly judging you, and worrying about your sins, never afraid to turn you in to the elders for 'counselling', and the elders always ready to give council.

No, this wasn't an environment that either of us could have wanted. But that's what it would have been, plus dealing with the close confinement of life in a camper trailer, most likely. But when you're young and naïve, and you have a strong desire for romance, coupled with anticipation of the 'end times', you might consider such a life. I did, anyway.

And then one Sunday morning, I received a phone call. It was one of the few Sundays I'd been able to sleep in. My father often woke me around 7:00 a.m. on Sundays to bring me to work, where in the brisk cold we'd burn piles of brush that had built up during the hot and humid, mosquito-ridden forests of summer. After a night staying up late drinking Castillo's rum and coke, such work was far from desirable, even though I hadn't had a hangover yet.

Jeff Heimerman, who's Hebrew name was Zaphanyah, called me that Sunday morning and said, "Brandon, I called to let you know that you can no longer speak to Samantha. It's finished."

"Okay." I responded, and I didn't ask any questions.

"You know, sometimes, this is how things go, and Yahweh always has a plan for us."

It wasn't a shock to me, and like I said, it had been practically impossible for us to develop any sort of emotional involvement with one another. Also, there was my involvement with a girl from school who got all my attention, and this circumstance only permitted me to deepen my feelings for her.

SUBTLE HATRED

Throughout high school I played sports. My freshman year I did wrestling and cross-country, and when I went to Westwood High I was on the swim team. My parents didn't encourage sports, really, because it was such a "worldly activity". But I wanted to do sports, and since I wasn't able to leave the house on Saturdays, those sports were the only ones I was able to do without missing a lot of meets.

I had an interest in playing football, and I was probably bigger than average, so my peers always encouraged me to play. But this didn't go over well with my father. Whenever I talked about my friends, or doing things with them, his response was, "They don't care about you, and they're not your friends. They're evil and they will only bring you closer to sin."

It was a hard message to hear at that point, because by my second year at Westwood, the kids had given me another chance. It was obvious that they didn't hate me anymore.

Of course I got picked on here and there because of my quirks, but who doesn't? All and all, we were kids, and for the first time in my life, I felt like these friends had my back.

I started to realize how mixed the messages were, coming from the House of Yahweh. First there was this idea that they loved people, and had compassion for everyone, as if they were ready to forgive everyone. But then I was told how evil the Catholics were, and how evil homosexuals were. We were taught that these were the most evil types of people out there, and Yahweh's biggest enemies. So I went along with it, to some degree, like in the jokes that people shared amongst themselves.

However, it eventually started to dawn on me that this mindset was unfair. I started to see in my mind that these assumptions were simply inappropriate, and that homosexuality or Catholicism had nothing to do with measuring someone's supposed level of evil. Somehow, bits and pieces of gravel were being poured into the machine of my belief system, and logic itself was stopping the gears from turning smoothly.

I couldn't hate these people, and if I mentioned hate out loud I was told, "Don't hate them, we're not supposed to." But when the only thing we're taught is how evil they are, how are we to feel? What are we to think of them? Many who denied their hatred clearly demonstrated their capacity to hate, saying how these people deserved to burn, how homosexuals deserved to get AIDS, how they all deserved to get the diseases they didn't even know they had. And we were also told, "Those who leave the House of Yahweh will become homosexuals." So that the very homophobia they planted in us would later be used as another scare-tactic to keep us in. There was always all this talk of forgiveness and acceptance, but such a readiness to condemn.

I knew Catholics, and I knew at least one homosexual. Even at that time, I wasn't afraid to say to myself, "These are good people." My choir director, for example – some 'conservatives' in the local community shamed him over rumors, but I knew it didn't matter. He was a good person, and regardless of whatever rumor someone might spread about his sexuality, it had nothing to do with his interactions at school. I don't know why it didn't matter to me, but it didn't.

And the idea that Catholics were evil. It was a Catholic who encouraged my faith in the House of Yahweh, who said, "If this is what you believe, then you need to do it." And on top of that, he was also a good person. One who I intuitively knew I could trust. It's not that I didn't want to believe those teachings of hatred – it's just that I couldn't.

I WASN'T THE ONLY ONE

My close friend Edward was having tremendous difficulties as well, and his actions were getting him into much deeper trouble than Jake and I experienced at the time. Even though we went to confession, and even though we'd be scolded for our behaviors, we didn't change them. We kept on doing what we would've done anyway, then stood ready for the consequences. Ed was having similar difficulties – he also wanted to date girls outside of the cult. Why he and I bothered to actually confess these things must have boggled Jake's mind.

Every feast, we showed up with our baggage. Luggage that we had to unpack in front of two priests, in order to get scolded and made to feel guilty.

One day, Ed had it very rough. He was in tears. Despite our parallel problems, all of us (Ed, Jake and I) tried to encourage each other to keep the faith. Which is what I tried to do with Ed at that moment. He'd been sleeping with a girl from his hometown. It was an ongoing relationship, and something you'd expect for an 18-year-old.

But when he confessed it, the elders dug deep into him and told him that he "wasn't called". That was like saying that he didn't even belong in the House of Yahweh, as if all the time he'd spent there meant nothing. Ed had been ordained a deacon, at a fairly young age.

You see, his father was one of the elders who left when the sect broke off. So he lost his father and his youngest brother, and now two elders who hadn't even been in the

124

House of Yahweh as long as him were guiding him through his shame. I'd never seem him so hurt before. This was his last feast, and it would be years until I saw him again.

I sat next to him in a small tent and watched him cry. Looking back, I know that those weren't tears of shame, but rather tears of frustration, confusion, and the feeling of "What am I going to do next?" He was ready to make the next step, and he knew he had to.

Ed came into the House of Yahweh before Jake and I did. He really was the third leg to our tripod, and without him there, it was like a piece of ourselves wasn't there. He was the first close friend that either of us had seen leave.

Of course, Jake and I visited other people and we had other friends, but Ed had been with us the longest, and we'd been with him the longest. We all had our own struggles, and when they hurt, we were all more or less honest with each other about it. Perhaps we might have been more honest with the priest than other teens were, and in the end, that honesty still worked out for the best.

FROM GOSSIP

About three months after I received that phone call from my counselor about not speaking to Samantha, I had a conversation with another friend down in Texas named Jones. Jones and I often spoke on instant messenger via computer. He asked me if I'd heard any news about Samantha, and I said no. He said I shouldn't repeat what he was going to tell me, and that he wasn't even supposed to know what had happened. How he learned it is still beyond me, although all the information turned out to be true.

Jones was the type of guy who seemed to be always 'in the know'. Why he bothered knowing all that gossip is also beyond me. In some ways I found it distasteful, but when you're young, what can you really be judged for? Jones was kind, but the alpha-male type, very like me, and like most of the guys in my circles of friends, both inside and outside the cult. He always seemed to have a mischievous smile that carried its own tone.

We spoke via internet and he told me that Samantha had gotten married. I wasn't sure what his motives were for telling me this, but I thought there was a chance that he was trying to make me jealous. So I inquired as to the situation, and he insisted that I wasn't to tell anyone, not my father, not my friends. He also said that he couldn't tell me everything, but that he'd fill me in more the next time I came to Texas.

So Samantha was married. She was 15 at the time, maybe 16. I'm not sure, but she was definitely younger than

18. She had married Yisrayl (Bill) Hawkins.

My reaction was more or less nonchalant. I didn't really care because I didn't have a lot of emotional involvement in her. But what concerned me was what Jones claimed not to be able to tell me at that time. I was curious to know more.

At this point, Bill allegedly had more than 30 wives. Women of all different ages, but most of them young. He was 70, so the only thing I found weird was that he was so old, and Samantha was so young. Yes, it did disgust me somehow, although I didn't let it get to me much. After all she had married the Overseer, and because of that, she'd have a guaranteed ticket into the Kingdom of Heaven.

All Jones told me then was that she'd married and who she'd married, plus the idea that she'd have a ticket into the Kingdom of Heaven as a result. Bill was affluent, and everyone knew it. He drove around in nice cars, wore linen suits, had several houses. Bill had money – more money than anyone else in his cult.

CULT EVOLUTION

The cult started getting strange. After confession came the burkas, and came the separation, and soon Yisrayl would be known as our king.

"He is our King!" Jeff Heimerman told me. I'll get back to that later.

Then there was the sacrifice of the heifer – a bizarre ritual that was known to us all. It was meant to cleanse us all from the dead.

According to the Bible, when anyone comes in contact with a dead body, or remains within the same area or room as a dead body, they'll be unclean until the water and ashes are sprayed on them from barley leaves by a priest. In order to do this, they would sacrifice a cow, burn its body, and mix its ashes with water. Then the priests would say a prayer, dip barley leaves into the ash water and wick it at the person who needs cleansing. At the time, this demonstration of superstition was written off simply because the leaders told us all it was what we needed. Of all the organized and practiced rituals that the House of Yahweh came up with, this was most likely the spookiest of all.

It went like this: all of us are unclean because of the dead. If you're a child and have never been around a dead body, you're still unclean because of your parents, or your parents' parents. There's no way of getting around it, like with STDs. Everyone in the House of Yahweh was told they had STDs. We were all told that no matter what, we needed to cleanse ourselves, both physically and spiritually.

Spiritually, we could cleanse by means of confession, and by adherence to the laws of Yahweh and the commandments given by our 'King'. Remember, these commandments could change as different individuals interpreted the behaviors of our 'King'. Like with the drinking of salt water.

Physically, we cleansed ourselves through the endless consumption of supplements, endless bottles of the latest 'soon to be trends' on the market. And it was odd to watch. Looking back, whatever the House of Yahweh told us we had to buy soon turned out to be the hottest health foods available. The House of Yahweh would tell us we needed to do a cleanse, or use a certain product, and then within a couple of years, it was actually a popular thing to do.

Young Living oils, for instance: we saw their prices rise drastically, and soon after, those products were available everywhere. Then there was the Colon Cleanse by Doctor Schultz, and all the other supplements, vitamins, herbs, and cleanses that went mainstream, including coconut oil. I assure you that the House of Yahweh preached about these first.

I would hear people talking about them in a tone that they really believed was scientific. Yisrayl assured us that he had scientists behind all of this research, and we never questioned it. We just took it as truth. None of us were scientists. We wanted to believe that we were, somehow, but we were only able to take the information given to us. We were encouraged to believe it was scientific, and that it was truth.

Sharing any of this cutting-edge cult-science with the public always raised eyebrows. People of certain wit knew to stay away, and people of weak logic would listen.

4. BUILDING ARMOR

I was a senior in high school when I started a short-lived hobby. A good friend of mine who brought a sincere amount of excitement into my life introduced me to chainmail. Tom and I had spent a lot of time with each other. We'd travel to nearby towns, take part in simple mischief like any pair of young boys might, and share many laughs. He was a significant part of my life, and he added energy to mine. Tom gave me an introduction to making chainmail – a technique for building armor that was hundreds of years old. And because I have obsessive tendencies, I quickly got hooked on creating items made from chainmail.

That was right before my senior year, and I recall being at the feast of Tabernacles in the early fall when I showed my friend Jake my new hobby. He showed moderate interest, but we were both more concerned with the fact that Ed wasn't with us at the feast. It was our first feast without him, and Jake was upset. I couldn't blame him. We both missed Ed. After that feast was when I knew I had to confront the elders about the situation with Samantha, and before that, I prepared. This preparation came so naturally, it still surprises me.

Once I'd learned about chainmail, I became obsessed. I would sit on my bedroom floor with my pliers, wire cutters and rings. I found myself thinking about nothing but only connecting the rings. I built two significant pieces of armor.

The first piece was called a 'coif', a head covering to

protect the head and neck of a soldier. I was commissioned to build it by the Vice Principal of my high school, who wanted it for his son as a Christmas present. The second piece took quite some time, but it protected the core of the body, and most importantly, the heart. I didn't build this all by myself. Tom and I worked on it together. We had discussed its construction and thought about different ways we might implement design. The piece was heavy, and intended for battle. We used 14-guage steel, so it was strong enough to withstand impact from a sword. Tom and I tested it with his authentic cavalry sword.

As I pursued my interest in building chainmail, I also built items out of brass, steel, copper, and silver. I made armor, I made jewelry, I made random sculptures. I was eager to show everyone the progress that I was making on my projects. I couldn't resist getting the approval. Certainly, a lot of my classmates found it annoying, but I couldn't help myself. This trait of seeking approval is one that I still catch myself doing today. One day, at school I was walking down the hallway between classes. I saw my friend Matt and showed him the pieces to a project that I was working on. He looked directly in my eyes with a sense of curiosity and fascination, and then said with a soft and convincing tone, "Brandon, you're building armor."

I looked down at the pieces in my hands, completely oblivious to what he might have been implying and simply replied, "I know."

At the time, my attention was only focused on putting one ring on after another. Ring by ring, building my armor.

Shortly after that, I was on the road to Texas, and I knew in my gut that this would be the last time.

NO LOVE FROM A KING

I had communicated a bit more with the young man who told me about Samantha. He told me that there were some dark sides to her involvement with Yisrayl. At that time, I had deepened my feelings for my high school sweetheart. I thought I was ready to begin the end of my time in the cult. When I packed for that trip, I packed lightly. I had a good idea that it might be the last time I'd go there.

It was a long ride, but they all blend together in my mind. The Midwest is mainly flat, except the hills of Missouri where the roads are cut through sandstone. The sun is warm, and the ground is the color of sand. I made it to the feast grounds, and shortly after, I looked for Jake. He was the only one I wanted to see.

I knew Ed wouldn't be there, but Jake might be. I felt like I needed him, or rather I knew that I needed him. But he wasn't there. His father told me that he hadn't come. I walked back slowly from his father's Silver Bullet camper, back to the bus my father had turned into his dwelling space. I wanted to leave that minute. I wanted to walk off the feast grounds, walk the 30 miles to the bus station, and take a bus back home. I didn't want to be there anymore. But I stayed.

I hadn't learned the details behind Samantha's marriage, but I would soon. Samantha's father went to Yisrayl and asked him personally, "Why did you not ask me for permission to talk to my daughter?" (We were taught to do this. It's tradition, and done out of respect for the father.)

Yisrayl's response was, "I don't have to ask for your permission. I'm your King."

This blew the man's mind, and rumor had it that he was pretty upset. I was also upset, though it had nothing to do with Samantha. I knew the whole idea of multiple wives not for me. And this was one of the first aspects of the cult that I disagreed with, especially after this situation arose.

It was the feast of Passover, and before Yashuah's memorial ceremony I went to give my confession. I confessed in a way where I could describe my shortcomings, but which was vague enough so they had to use their imaginations. In hindsight they might have felt cheated, but it's what I did and it was righteous.

Somehow, I was beginning to grasp the simple mindset that they all seemed to work with. I was able to take their whole realm of logic and see it in the palm of my hand. However, my biggest battle at that point was to be sure, and to endure. I needed to ask questions and let them tell me in their own answers, to clarify that it was okay for me to leave. I needed to allow them to expose their own flaws. Not only that, I needed to keep it to myself, because it wasn't my responsibility to convince anyone else that this place was wrong. I knew I had to keep that to myself.

After my last confession and Yashuah's memorial, we had the Seder meal. We were all dressed in black and white suits, and we had all finished our eight glasses of wine.

We were waiting in line for our food, and I made sure that I'd be in the right line to be served by Yisrayl Hawkins.

There I was, getting closer and closer. I stared at him,

waiting for his eyes to connect with mine. Still, I knew he knew I was coming. When I arrived, I looked at him, I looked him in his eyes and said, "May Yahweh bless your marriage with Samantha."

Breaking his eye contact swiftly, he looked down and pretended like he hadn't heard me. So I said it again, with a little more strength in my voice, "May Yahweh bless your marriage with Samantha." And he still wouldn't make eye contact. He only stared to the floor on his right side. Almost out of fear, it seemed.

What a coward, I thought. And with the nerve to convince everyone that he was King, and to take praise from everyone as if he really were.

A few days passed, and within that time I told my father what I had done. He didn't have much of an answer, but a couple of days later Jeff Heimerman spoke to me. He scolded me, and he said, "Of course he wouldn't acknowledge you, why should he? And how dare you say that to him. He is our King, and whatever he says goes. He will not be judged for it. He is our King, and we need to accept everything he does."

In my thoughts, I said to myself, "This is all I needed to hear. That's it, and now I can be done with it." I responded to Jeff, "Thank you for telling me this." And I smiled at him.

He said calmly, "You know, Brandon, we just need to follow Yahweh's laws as they're presented to us by the chosen one. That's it."

I said, "You're right." I nodded my head in pretended

agreement, and walked away casually.

That moment was the most difficult of my life to that point. Not only did I want to leave, but I didn't want to affect anyone else. So I had to pretend. Just for a few more days.

I simply didn't feel it was my role to share my feelings with those around me. I felt as if it were my burden alone, and when it came time for others to make a similar decision, they would. I just knew that it wasn't up to me.

Much of this time, I sat by myself, wearing my holy garments with my arms crossed in the sanctuary. I just wanted time to pass. I just wanted to go home to face my next obstacle. Once, Gary Matilla stopped by me and said, "You know, you're so strong for still being here. Your friends are gone, but you're still here."

I nodded and continued to sit there, wrapped in my "holy garments" and staring off into the distance of the sanctuary.

THE LAST RETURN

My father, Linda and I returned to Michigan, and the feast of Pentecost was only 50 days away. At this point, I knew that I was never going to go back to the House of Yahweh. I was done with it. There was no way I could possibly believe it was the right thing to follow. And at this point, it wasn't a question of whether they were right or wrong, righteous or evil, the one way to salvation or not. I simply didn't care. I said to myself in my heart, "I disagree with Yisrayl Hawkins so much, I'm willing to burn quietly in hell for it."

We got back from Texas and I was ready to go back to school and start my own routine. To see my friends, about whom my father had said, "They're not your friends, they don't care about you." To spend time with my girlfriend and feel less guilty about it, and to prepare for a life that I had never planned on having.

I even went to prom, which was difficult to pull off without my father getting upset. I had taken care of getting the suit ready. My mother helped me, and she helped organize other aspects of being able to go. Prom was on a Saturday, and leaving the house before Sunset would be difficult to do. I knew it would cause a confrontation between my father and myself, but I also knew that my father would give in, and that he ultimately couldn't stop me.

I lied to him and told him I was going for a drive, and that I'd be spending the night at my mother's house.

Instead I was planning to go to prom, and then stay in a hotel room with my date. To be honest, nothing really happened in the hotel room, other than innocent cuddling and two teens watching movies.

Time passed quickly. It was my senior year of high school and the feast of Pentecost was quickly approaching. Soon I'd have to make the move. Soon I'd have to make the hardest decision of my life, which would set me free.

Freedom sounds grand. It sounds wonderful, something everyone wants. A wider spectrum will reveal a fuller range of possibilities. But many possible outcomes can be difficult to accept at a young age, at least subconsciously.

The time came for me to break the news to my father. I was organizing my belongings in my bedroom, and I mentioned to my father that I didn't want to go down for the next feast. He'd been in the hallway, walking past my bedroom door, and he came into my room to further this conversation.

I told him that I didn't agree with the teachings. I told him that I didn't agree with the fact that Yisrayl Hawkins was immune to sin, and could do whatever he pleased. I told him that Hawkins didn't have the right to be disrespectful to people, regardless of whether he was the chosen one or not. I also told him that I'd rather burn in the Lake of Fire than to keep on following this religion.

My father looked me in the eyes with his fingers pointed down and his palms facing me and said, "You're committing spiritual suicide."

I responded with, "I don't agree with it. It's better for

me to be apart from you than to follow something I don't believe in."

Right after we spoke about me leaving the house of Yahweh, my father knew he couldn't change my mind. He knew that something needed to be worked out. He said, "Well I suppose you will have to stay here while we go to Texas, but I will need to ask David Heimerman first, to see if that's okay."

He called David Heimerman and came back upstairs to my bedroom to tell me that the elders said I couldn't stay at the house, and that I had a week to get out. My response was with a lifted eyebrow, "Really?"

My father replied, "David Heimerman told me to kick the asshole out of the house right now." Also that no one was expecting that I planned on leaving the House of Yahweh so suddenly. But I knew that they wouldn't expect it. I knew by then the facade they wanted to see, and the truth is, all of them were easily fooled. Just as easily fooled as others were when Yedidyah Hawkins (now in prison for child molestation) told them that they could pretty much do whatever they wanted, as long as they paid their tithes.

I already had a bag packed, and when my father relayed to me what his "counselor" told him to do, I grabbed the bag and I left. I had no idea where to go.

I was still in high school, with a little bit more to go. I guess you could say I did what any young boy would do in this situation. I went to my mother's house.

I tossed my backpack on the passenger seat of my red 1985 Ford Ranger, and headed to the outskirts of

Marquette. I called my mother and told her what I had done, and she said she was very glad, and she told me I needed to come over. I said I was already on my way.

"Great honey. I'm so happy." She said cheerfully.

I showed up at the house with my backpack over one shoulder, and I opened the screen door and walked in. "How are you?"

"I'm okay," I replied.

"I just got a package in the mail with a new coffee table in it. Could you put it together for me?"

"Yeah, okay."

I sat on the floor and built her furniture. I recall a few boxes of items bought from a catalogue. She stayed in the kitchen while I worked in the living room. The feeling of loneliness was so strong and so numbing that I didn't even realize it was there.

Shortly after that, I left. I went to spend the night at a friend's house, where I slept on his floor. We didn't stay up very late because we had school the next day.

During the morning before class, I was walking into the school, and that's when I saw Mr. Bradley. I walked up to him as we were heading into school and said, "I told my father that I didn't want to be a part of the House of Yahweh anymore."

"What did he say?" he asked.

"He kicked me out of the house."

"Oh no, Brandon, if you need any help, I'm here for you."

"I'll be okay. Thank you."

FINISHING HIGH SCHOOL

I had roughly one month before high school finished. It was my senior year, and I didn't have much to worry about, academically. What was done was done. I had a C-minus grade point average. I suppose it wasn't all that bad, considering the trips I took to Texas three times during the school year.

My excuse was, "Well hey, I thought the world was going to end."

But no one asked me about it anyway. The good part was, I was getting a high school diploma.

My friend Kyle and I had teamed up together before this all happened and started a petition to excuse the senior class from taking final exams. We thought that we were well-organized on paper, and the petition changed hands and just about everyone was on board. Only a few teachers were opposed to it, but eventually, we were able to get the entire senior class out of taking final exams, in all of our classes. We'd already had 'final' exams throughout high school anyway, and what was one extra set when most of us had already been accepted into college?

That was a bright note in my senior year. Aside from that, I needed to find a place to live. Sleeping at friends' houses or in the back of my truck in the school parking lot could only last so long. I couldn't stay at my mother's house, with her fiancé. Not because I wasn't allowed to, but because the household dynamic was the same as when I was a child. I couldn't handle it, especially at that point in my life. I felt as if there was no way to get help from my parents unless I lived a life that they expected me to live, which was completely irrational on both sides.

My mother's fiancé was into real estate. He would buy low-end properties, fix them up a tiny bit and then rent them out for the average price typical of the area. To make a long story short, he didn't have the best reputation in the community. However, he knew someone who had an apartment for rent in a triplex. It was a one-bedroom place, a bit run down. The entrance door didn't work, but I knew I could fix that and probably get my rent lowered for one month.

About a week before high school graduation I moved into that apartment. I paid a security deposit and the first five weeks of rent.

My girlfriend at the time knew that the door didn't work, and one day I came home and realized that her and her mother had bought me nearly a month's worth the food, a toaster, and other kitchen supplies.

"What a nice thing to come home to," I thought.

ALONE

High school graduation came, and I was ready to start the summer. I had a job doing landscaping for some of my father's clients, but I knew that would last for only so long.

I wouldn't be able to work near my father, especially without arguing. And when you argue with someone who's in a cult, you end up arguing against circular reasoning, or something like a wall, without logic (although I didn't really understand this at the time). The feelings that I had for my father weren't hateful, but rather deep frustration for the fact that he would do what he was told so unquestioningly, from someone who had never truly showed any interest in his well-being.

I remember one time the House of Yahweh had overcharged him for dues on his trailer, by several thousand dollars, and he needed that money. David Heimerman told him, "Why not just give it as a free-will offering?" As if it wasn't a lot, or he didn't need it.

Basically, he was told that nothing was more important than paying in money to the cult.

Yes, I was frustrated that my father would listen to this goon, and yet so easily let go of his own son. I never would have thought that letting go of a child could be so easy. For some parents it's possible, and for others it would never cross their minds. Only someone in such a strong sect with severe mind control could do this.

I understood the dynamics of the House of Yahweh, and when it came to "fall-aways", as we leavers were known

– we were the most evil of all. We were those who knowingly rejected the teachings of the cult. It was something no one else could understand, unless they'd been in my shoes. I was alone, separated from my immediate family, and from anyone who might truly understand what I was dealing with. People often handed me answers, as if they knew a solution.

But it was easy to know who to listen to, and that was no one, because anyone who had any answers didn't know anything. It was frustrating and confusing, and it was just the beginning of what I'd have to deal with emotionally as time went on. The best type of advice has always been given to me in the form of metaphor and rhetoric. For this I owe gratitude to my lifelong mentors.

My father never showed up to my graduation. Maybe he was told not to by the elders, or the "Kahans", as they started calling themselves shortly before I left. An imp is still an imp, call it what you want.

Maybe my father decided that on his own. I remember opening graduation cards from my friends, sister, brother, mother, and being overwhelmed with emotion for the financial help I was getting. I received about $500, and that would surely help me get through the next month while I looked for another job.

THE SUMMER BEFORE UNIVERSITY

June 13th came around, and I was hired at one of the main hardware stores in Marquette. I had a lot of experience in the trades, and that seemed to be the trick in getting hired. Perhaps all those weekends and Christmas days spent in the woods with my father paid off.

The pay was a little higher than average at the time, around $7/ hour. I got around 30 hours a week on average, enough to make ends meet, paying for my apartment and other bills. I needed the job, and my mother helped with my persistence in getting it. Probably thanks to her, I had the talking skills to succeed in the interview.

The summer went by fast. I spent most of it working, trying to figure out what I was going to do when college started. I was considering buying the triplex that I lived in and the duplex next door. The owner of the buildings had offered me a good deal to buy them on a 'land contract'. My mother's fiancé was also interested in the buildings, and that became another variable in our relationship. He was strongly opposed to me buying the buildings, even though he had encouraged me years before to "get into real estate".

It seemed pretty obvious to me that he was more concerned with his empire of slum-shacks than anything else. I was pretty close to signing the contract. The owner would've rather done business with me than with my mother's fiancé, but if I didn't sign the contract, the owner would sell them to him. He just needed to get rid of the buildings.

As the summer ended, I was preparing to organize my classes for my first semester of university. I didn't know what I wanted to do, but I knew that I should do something with music. My grades were low coming out of high school, which didn't look good to many professors on campus.

I went to the music department and spoke with the head of the program, Donald Grant. He was stand-off-ish and didn't seem to think I'd be a good fit for the program, because of my high school grades. We were standing in a temporary office of his, an older music classroom. An entirely new music building was being built. I asked whether I could play the piano, and he said sure and told me to go right ahead.

I started playing the Tempest Sonata by Beethoven, and he stood behind his desk, in pause, holding his papers in his left hand. I stopped playing and said, "I'm still working on this."

His response was, "We need to get you into this music program."

MUSIC HISTORY

All the practicing I had done on the piano throughout my childhood got my foot in the door with the music department at our local university. I didn't really see it as a huge accomplishment, but it set the trajectory for the rest of my college years. Dr. Grant sold me on the music education program. He was a good salesman in that regard, and this I let slip by me.

How I was going to pay for all this was beyond me. My father had already filled out the paperwork for financial aid, so what I could get would be based on his income. He surely wouldn't help me to go to college now. He had been more or less against the idea anyway.

I needed a co-sign for a student loan, so I was told that I should ask my mother. I told the office that she wouldn't do it, because of her previous debt experience. They said that it didn't matter, and I could still get aid if she didn't qualify. She just needed to fill out the paperwork.

So I went to my mother, knowing what her answer would be. I asked her, and she surprised me by saying, "Maybe you don't need to go to college."

I was stunned. She had told me my entire life that I needed to go to college. And now, when the time of truth had arrived, this was the answer I received. There were no ifs, ands, or buts about it. She wouldn't have anything to do with that paperwork. She convinced me at that point that I would never have her to fall back on, in any way.

I returned to the financial aid office, explaining what

had happened. I had also previously told them of my situation with the cult. I was told that they were investigating that, but I would still have to pay for the first semester out of pocket while they made their decision. How I would come up with over four thousand dollars was beyond me. I didn't even have money to buy textbooks.

I went through the semester without textbooks. I had several classes a week, and music courses were more time-consuming than anything. They weren't worth many credits, so a full-time schedule could easily make for a 40-hour school week. Meanwhile I worked morning shifts at the hardware store before classes.

My typical day was to get up around 3:30 or 4:00 a.m., work for four hours, go to class until 9:00 p.m., and get to bed around 10. It was exhausting, and barely enough to get by. I still lived in Ishpeming, and the drive between there and Marquette was very time-consuming. Some nights were spent in dorm rooms, in my car, on couches, or in a sleeping bag on the beach. That was incredibly tiring, and soon I would need to find a way to move to Marquette so I wouldn't have to commute any longer.

HOW I LEARNED STRENGTH

Just before time was about to run out on paying my bill to the university, I came across a glitch on a website selling computer parts. Someone on their end had added an extra zero on a discount item, and when I went to check out, it put my balance into the negative (as in, they owed me money). In the end I was able to get a lot of computer parts and other electronics at a very cheap price. Within a month I had resold these items on Ebay and made the four thousand that I needed to pay to the university.

I was feeling more confident about my situation. My grades were the best they'd ever been, and I was meeting new people. I could actually feel my mind opening up. There were so many things about life and society in general that I had been held back from.

One early afternoon, I decided that I was ready to talk to my mother. I was ready to tell her about the things that I had felt separated us, and that had played a big part in the downfall of our relationship. I felt that getting these things off my chest would make me feel better, and potentially put us on better terms. I didn't want to fight about these things, but they needed to be talked about, if only because they had never been talked about.

I sat on a bench in the sun outside Bookworld on Washington Street. I called my mother and said that we needed to talk. She said that she thought that would be a good idea.

I said that there were things bothering me, and she said

that there were things bothering her, too. I brought up the time when she told my father and me that she would open a bank account to help fund my college expenses. She told us this back when she was with her third husband.

She responded with denial. I expected that, so I let it go. And then I brought up the time when I was taken to the doctor, right before my father was to take custody of me, when I was a young boy. I asked her how the idea of me being molested had come about, and I told her how much it had really bothered me. I asked her why she took me to the doctor, and how it led to her regaining custody of me. The conversation dragged on through denial, approached gaslighting and ended in verbal violence.

"You're a stubborn fucking Finlander. You're just like you're fucking father. Fuck you, you stubborn fucking Finlander."

It was something that I needed to hear. One last push so I could pick myself up and continue on my independent journey. I hung up the phone, choking on my tears. I left the bench, headed to campus, and sat under a tree.

I could only think of one person to call. One person who wouldn't throw clearly defined answers at me, but who would just empathize. "Beeg!" (Referring to B.G. my high school English teacher.) I said after he picked up the phone. I told him what happened, and he listened.

We had our conversation, and I was able to pick myself up again. I headed to the library to get back to studying. I knew I wouldn't talk to my mother again for a long time. I knew I needed to protect myself from her. I couldn't ask anything from her, and I couldn't talk about anything with her, especially if this was how it would end. I had too many confusions to deal with to bring that into my life.

By the time I arrived at the library, my tears had dried. I felt exhausted, but yet I felt like I had some type of high. I looked away from the library entrance, toward a large grassy area. The water sprinklers had just been turned on. A girl sitting on a bench outside the library entrance looked up at me through her glasses and said "Wouldn't it be nice to run through the sprinklers?" And without hesitation, I picked her up ran her through the water. We looked at each other, smiling and laughing. I returned to the entrance, sat her back down where she was sitting, and proceeded to enter the library soaking wet.

5. A BIGGER BOX

College, paired with the aftershocks of an unstable childhood, led to a new normal: partying, sex, marijuana, anxiety, and depression. I wasn't the only one who had these issues. There were others who had left the House of Yahweh, and like me, found themselves crying into a telephone because they couldn't make sense of all the psychological pain and confusion. It was a transitional stage, and one that no one could ever prepare for. A college professor of mine, Dr. Englehart, used the metaphor of a pendulum to describe something similar. The idea was that when a pendulum is lifted, it has the inertia to swing into another realm before it comes back and eventually discovers equilibrium. "It will be interesting to see where you end up." He said humbly.

I could go on and on about the details of my college years, but partying is partying. Meaningless sex has all the weight of meaningless arguments. It was rather the vicious cycle of drugs, sex, alcohol and depression that I ignored. My ego didn't allow me to see the connections. I'll mention the subtle feeling of guilt that always followed climax during those years. It reminds me of Pavlov's bell in some ways.

Years of lessons from the cult, training one's mind and emotions how and when to work. It's hard for me to believe that they told us we'd become homosexuals if we were to ever leave. As if that was supposed to scare me away from leaving?

At times I would jokingly say, "I'm only waiting to find

out I'm gay." Sarcasm helped push the annoyances of my history aside, but watching my mother's relationships from the sidelines, coupled with the bizarre marriage rituals of the cult, created heavy complications that frustrated my understanding of how relationships might actually work. Guilt, fear, and confusion would be the obstacles I would have to overcome through my college years and then some.

In the cult we were taught to worry about the future of the world, the fragility of our health, the likelihood of STDs and nuclear war. It was like growing up with FOX news in the background yelling, "Death, War, Famine, AIDS!" I can hear comedian Bill Hicks' voice saying those words. Except in the cult, you don't know it's just FOX news – you don't know it's not real.

Although it was nice to be health conscious, this was taken to extremes. Drinking too much colloidal silver and doing too many liver cleanses can't be very healthy, either. And even though some of these worries sound fallacious, the subconscious impact they had on my psyche drove me mad at times. My mind and body needed to readjust to a reality that I was striving to discover on my own.

I had to re-learn human interaction. I had to discover for myself that the behaviors both my parents taught me were not as commonplace as I once believed. I needed to find myself, to discover the beliefs and values that I would choose to hold dear – independently. The meaning in life that I wanted to believe in, and not what someone told me I needed to believe in, just because we shared a certain level of DNA, or because it was written down somewhere a long time ago an accepted as fact. This meant that I would start searching for my own path through life, a path where I would wander for years in self-discovery, often finding myself with these words: "Ah, nope, not yet. You might have thought so, but not just yet." I still pass over these words now with that same feeling.

EMOTIONAL CONFUSION

Loneliness weighed heavy throughout college, as it had in my early years. But I was an adult now, and I had my own place to go back to. I learned how to cook, I kept my place clean and organized. I wanted to be a good partner for someone; I wanted to find someone.

I sought out romance. I gave whatever I could that I thought girls might want. Most girls found me weird, some crazy, but the wise ones could clearly see that I was lost. And they held a safe distance while still sharing compassion. They were my friends, and still are, and they watched me change. Just like the male counterparts in our group. Yes, in college we meet life-long friends. They inspire us, and we do all we can to make ourselves better because of that.

I entered into relationships fast, and I got burned as often as I burned others. There were times I was used by women, which only led to me to contemplate my past. "How can all this change?" I thought to myself. And then I met a woman with whom I fell heavily in love. It was during my sophomore year of college. She was tall, beautiful, British, cute in a typical girly way with proper nails and makeup. She was the first woman I lived with, and after we split up, it was the hardest breakup to deal with.

We weren't right for each other, but that didn't matter at the time, because I couldn't understand how. That would take quite some time. What I did realize, though, was that the romance I had dumped into the relationship was fake, and built on fantasy. It may have made things fun to a certain degree, but in the end it was like building a house on sand. And that was something that I would be certain to never do again.

Unfortunately, this practice played a huge role in my next relationship. A blonde woman who I met through the music department who showed interest in me around the time that the British woman and I were splitting up. She was as young and confused as I was, and to a great degree, she wanted the fantasy that I wanted, too. But because she was a little younger, we didn't see things on the same level. We dated on and off for the remainder of college.

We travelled together, cooked meals together, fought together, and in some ways grew together. We lived together at the end of our segmented relationship, and that was the last time we were together. It was an odd relationship in some ways, but special too. It taught me a very special thing about relationships: that people will always be who they themselves intend to be.

One day, in Ecuador, she told me (laughing at the end), "Brandon, when I'm 27 or so, I'm going to get married. I'm not waiting any longer than that. I hope it's with you, but if not, then it is what it is. That's what I'm going to do."

And that was when I knew that I wouldn't be the one for her.

REFINING WHAT'S RIGHT

Intentions were the one thing that stuck with me as time went on. I always had good intentions. Don't get me wrong, there were many times that I acted selfishly or cruel, but it was out of fear and unawareness. As I realized my flaws, I changed them, and that is what I believe good intentions to be all about.

I hadn't spoken with my mother in quite some time. It was my third year of college, and my brother would often question why. Looking back, I couldn't expect him to understand. I had been hurt enough by her, and I was still resentful of the way she treated me. But eventually we started talking again, and when we did, it was as I expected – pretending that nothing had ever happened. Smiles and exaggerated laughter.

My brother and I lived across the hall from each other, and the family was having pizza there. After we ate, I invited my cousin and mother over to my apartment for coffee. I was proud of my well-kept apartment. Nice things were situated throughout. I felt sophisticated to a large degree, although at that time I was just beginning to let go of that illusion.

I had a large bookshelf, recycled from the university, and on it were various trinkets, vases, and large coffee-table books. Since I'd been given most of those things for free, or had paid very little for them, any time guests would come over, I'd tell them that they could have anything on the bookshelf. Whatever they wanted.

It was and still always is a good feeling to give something away.

When I made the same gesture to my cousin and my mother, both wanted the same vase. My mother said, "Nope, I wanted it first." I had to bite my tongue. They agreed that if she didn't want it at some future point, she would give it to my cousin.

My cousin had it hard, too. She was moved around as a child and experienced social prejudice that few ever experience, not knowing who she might be accepted by. She was like my little sister, though she was almost the exact same age as me. We had a lot of similarities. So many, it caused us to not get along at times. Looking back, I can see that the most difficult moments of our lives were also very similar.

My family and I had coffee at my place. I believe I played piano for all of them. Then after that, we went back to my brother's apartment to continue our visit. Nothing was serious. There was no fighting or bickering – nothing felt empty, but nothing felt full. My brother and I had a bond, and from that point on, the bond would continue to grow. He was already a father, a man. I was still young, but scars from my past gave me a peculiar edge. We were finally able to engage in deeper dialogue and begin to open up to each other.

COLLEGE FLEW BY

I was nearing my 4th year of college, and the interest I'd developed in jazz was firmly set. A year before I had met a couple of guys who were performing at a bar. I'd heard about Dane Bays before: I was told by many that I should talk to him about music.

At the bar where he was playing, I spoke to him with a hint of arrogance. He didn't have many words, but the words that he did have were, "You want to play? What do you want to play?"

I asked if he knew 'On Green Dolphin Street' and said that I could probably read the chart if he had one.

"Ok, lets play 'On Green Dolphin Street'."

The truth is, my arrogance and naiveté put me in a position where I didn't know what I was getting myself into. I sat at the keyboard and I couldn't keep up. At all. The truth is, I couldn't play anything at the standard of Dane Bays and Alex Brooks. These guys were killing it, and they weren't going to hold back to hold my hand.

After we were done, Dane said to me, "If you want to learn how to play jazz, come to my house on Tuesday."

So I did. I went to his house then, and whenever he offered. Often twice a week. I did what he told me to do. I learned why singing with the music was important, I learned emotional intent, and I learned time. Musical qualities that hadn't been stressed in the Music School. Before long, people started to notice that within 6 months of learning under Dane and Alex, my playing was transformed, and as far as I could tell, Donald Grant didn't like what was happening.

"Brandon," Dane told me, "you're the only person that kept coming. That's what's different about you. Later Jon came, and you two are the only people who kept coming. No one else would."

Jon was a bass player who Dane encouraged me to bring over. We both shared great interest in jazz, and that's what created our friendship. Little did we know that jazz would make our Music Department experiences very similar.

I can't speak for Jon, because he has his own words, but my story is very similar to his. Without a doubt, my musical progress throughout university was something to be proud of, but thanks to my training, it taught me more humility than pride. Not only did I tackle difficult classical pieces, but I started the path of bebop – something incredibly difficult, and not taught at the university. My piano professor was incredibly kind and encouraging, and she stuck with me until the very end.

I can't be dishonest about my behavior in the music department. I was most definitely a smart-ass, and the conservative atmosphere in the department fueled most of my comments. However, towards the end of my 4th year, I had my final piano proficiency exam. I played my scales, the 3rd movement to the Moonlight Sonata, and I sight-read. My sight-reading was definitely the weakest, but still not terrible. The next weekday I got my results back and it said "re-take." Which was common, but it meant I would need to spend another entire year before I could re-do it. I was pissed – it didn't make sense, especially considering other kids who had already graduated. I didn't talk about it to anyone for a week.

At my next piano lesson, I spoke with my teacher. She seemed happy. I told her that I failed and her jaw nearly dropped. She said she couldn't believe that I had failed. She quickly grabbed the papers out of filing cabinet, only to find that the one deciding paper that determined whether I had passed or failed was missing. I went to Donald Grant, and his only response as he walked away was, "The papers were there."

I told my piano teacher that was I going to change majors. She encouraged it, and said that she probably would too, in a similar circumstance. Shortly after that, I was walking down the hallway near the recital hall where the jazz festival was being held. An African-American man walked in the main entrance. He was a famous jazz trombonist who was paid to be there by the university. Donald Grant walked by him and said, "Please take off your hat." And he walked away.

ACADEMIC SHIFT

I switched my major to Sociology at the end of my 4th year in college. Unexpectedly, college was easy sailing after this. My humor was accepted, my sarcasm fit, my grades got even higher, and I became good friends with almost the entire faculty. Still to this day.

It took nearly five years for my anxiety to fade into something I felt I could control. Which isn't to say that it still didn't affect me. As always, I continued to experience feelings of worry in my teeth and in my stomach. The subtle color of anxiety frequently tickled the roots in my gums, and when something discomforting struck quickly, my stomach would twist like a shirt caught in a drill. My peers were all worried about what they would do after college, but I wasn't. It's not that I knew what I was going to do – I was just preoccupied with keeping my emotions and thoughts under rational control.

I was so much closer to control than I had ever been. I often looked back to when I was 19 or 20.

Back then, I was in great shape. I could bench-press my bodyweight 15 times. I could drink like a tank and still speak like a shark, but my level of insecurity was through the roof. I had no idea how to accept myself, and as a result I struggled with accepting others.

I always felt the need to prove myself back then. Not because I wanted to be better than my peers, but because I didn't know how to be comfortable with myself. There were times that I would smoke spliffs like cigarettes on the way to class. I kept them in a pill jar inside my black leather coat. I did this partly because it was cool, but mainly because it provided some means of escape. If anything, it allowed me to have a different perspective on things, and at the time, that seemed to be what I needed. Of course I thought it was hidden well, but the faculty knew what was going on.

When I was 24, I knew I still hid behind some facades. I knew I still had a lot of growing to do. I wasn't as macho as I had been at 19 or 20. My substance-usage came under control, and my behavior became more refined as I looked up to those who showed me benevolence and compassion through example and their acceptance of me.

The bar scene died quickly for me. I was 24, and I'd been drinking at the local bars for six years. I still went to bars occasionally, but for the most part they bored me. As I started to learn more about jazz, and find comfort in academics, a great wave of relief fell over me and allowed me to feel guided into doing what I felt I needed to do. As ambiguous as this feeling was, I started to have faith in my actions.

It was at this age that I started to believe that there was nothing more important in my life than to have good intentions. Maybe it was jazz that started me on this line of thinking, or maybe it was my father, or maybe it was the naturally occurring swing of the pendulum. It doesn't matter. This was a new trajectory, and things were just beginning to get more exciting.

MY FIRST TRAVELS

In my 5th year of college, I managed to enroll in a course that would take me overseas. My partner at the time encouraged me to do it, and she helped with the logistics. I had been imagining for a few years what it was like 'over there', and for the most part I found out that I'd imagined it fairly well. What I imagined wasn't what you might expect for the first time traveler. Most of the time, imagining things was spent imagining how I'd accept my new surroundings, and maybe that was just what I needed to do, to ensure a great time.

The study-abroad course focused on French art history and architecture. We would start in Amsterdam, then travel to Brussels and to Paris. By this time, I had a grand interest in the art of Van Gogh and Picasso. I had some prints of their paintings hanging up in my apartment. In fact, a dentist who I did landscaping for showed me some 'original fakes' of their paintings, and his interest fostered mine.

It's probably not surprising that when I saw the real paintings by Van Gogh, I was floored. I even cried after staring at one of those paintings for a while. I couldn't believe that such tremendous, wizard-like things could be done with paint. I told myself at that moment that when I returned to the States, I would throw away all those prints and never take part in that nonsense again.

Aside from the art and the architecture, the energy that I felt from my surroundings was something that I couldn't have predicted at all. I'm not sure if it was me, or culture shock, but I felt like I belonged there. I felt free from judgement, free to express and explore. It was a great feeling, and the first time I'd ever felt it as an adult. Then I visited the Monet Gardens in France.

Monet's paintings never really spoke to me. I couldn't ever disregard his work, but I had greater interest in other painters like Bosch, Van Gogh, or Picasso. But when I saw his gardens, I saw that there was truly something special to what he had built. With all the exotic flowers, diversely and strategically placed throughout, I had an overwhelming sensation that reminded me of my stepmother, Linda.

Linda loved flowers. The memory of seeing her with flowers brings tears to my eyes. She was a simple lady in many ways. She was hard-working, loving, and with an astonishing ability to find great joy in the simple things in life. When I saw those flowers, I thought of her, and still whenever I think of those flowers, I think of her.

As I've said before, Linda and I had a very difficult relationship, and it wasn't until shortly after leaving the cult that I realized how our relationship had been tainted because of the religion. She was subject to so much control. How she treated her body, or what she'd been taught about how others would view her presence simply because she was a woman. She was taught to believe that she was unclean all the time, and because of that, she had to do more work than men in order to be saved. Linda was sweet, with a heart full of honesty, and the Monet gardens brought me back to the memory of her.

166

NO DOCTORS NEEDED

I returned from Europe after a short but packed trip, visiting three countries. It was a blast, and now it was time to enjoy the summer.

Shortly after my return, I had a piano gig booked for a private party at a local popular venue. Earlier in the day before the gig, I decided to play basketball with my brother. We were playing two-on-two with a couple of guys who just got out of the joint. Needless to say, they'd probably had a bit more practice in the recent past than we had. Then it happened, in the middle of the game, I jumped up to get a rebound and I landed on someone's foot the wrong way.

"Pop!" goes my ankle.

I dropped to the ground with concern. It didn't hurt, it was completely numb. That's how I knew it was bad.

"Shit, I have a gig today," I said out loud.

Some guys were playing tennis nearby, and they came over to double-check that I was okay. They even said they were going to be at the show later that night. Being surrounding by concerned people was nice, but there was nothing anyone could do. I tightened up my shoe, hopped on my bike, and coasted downhill back to my apartment.

I tried playing the piano when I got back with my left foot soaking in a bucket of ice water. Then the pain kicked in, and boy did it hurt. I needed to lay down. I called my partner, and she thankfully had some Motrin and a walking splint. She rushed to my aid, and the pain died down. I tried to make a couple of jokes, but I don't think they went across well. If it wasn't for her, this situation would have been incredibly difficult.

Later that night I went to the gig, and things turned out okay. The men who were playing tennis showed up and said, "So you went to the doctor?" I said that I hadn't, but I was able to manage.

I told them what I did and they said, "Well it seems like you knew what you were doing. The music sounds good."

I went home and then went to bed with the splint on. I woke up the next day and visited my brother in the morning. He asked if my ankle was okay, and I said it was.

He said, "You know, I don't like it when two guys wearing redneck boots beat us in basketball."

I will never forget him saying that.

It wasn't until almost 6 weeks later that it finally healed. My brother told me, "Good job on not going to the hospital."

Perhaps growing up with a disdain of the health system prevented me from doing so. I didn't have the money anyway, and I never went for a sprained ankle. This is how I was raised: we don't go to the hospital. My father never took me unless I needed stitches, and I never remember my stepmother or father going, ever. It's just the way things were.

THE TRAVEL ITCH

I'd begun to speak with my father again around this time. The summer before my last year of college, I was standing outside the public library, talking to him on the phone. "You know, I really think you should consider turning your ways back to Yahweh," he said.

"Dad, I will never turn my ways back to the House of Yahweh. Yisrayl Hawkins is a selfish and manipulative person, and I was sure when I told you before that I'd rather burn in hell than to follow his teachings."

"Well I still think you should reconsider," he said.

"It's not going to happen."

We didn't argue that time, but there was tension in our conversation. I was still frustrated with his endurance in the cult. I still hadn't accepted it by then, I still thought maybe there was some chance that my father would turn around and be among those who had selfless love for him; his family.

Our conversation ended and I went on with my evening. I felt like our communication might be starting to build again, but I didn't really start talking with him until several months after.

The first semester of my final year of college was a busy one. I studied harder than I ever had, and I put honest effort into pursuing my interest in jazz. I was taking difficult classes, but I found them fascinating. I had just one more difficult semester, and then an easy one, before I'd be done with school.

After that semester, my friend and jazz mentor offered me a room for rent in his house. There I could practice piano and continue learning. Because of this, and the price he offered, it was a deal that I couldn't refuse. It turned out to be a great decision, and my piano playing continued to get better.

That last semester I had a huge itch to travel again, and my significant other wanted me to visit her in Ecuador. She was doing her student teaching, and she thought it would be a good idea to visit her during spring break.

I figured, why not? I could take an extra week of school off and make up the work when I got back. I knew my Research Methods teacher wouldn't agree, but my peers and I had the idea that it was better to ask for forgiveness than permission in such a situation. I managed to get a ticket from Marquette to Quito, then to Atlanta (to visit my cousin) and then back to Marquette, for just $800. I thought it was a pretty good deal.

I had bought the ticket, and then right after that, I found out that Linda had come down with cancer. I was a bit concerned, and so was my family. I spoke with her over the phone, and she had nothing but kind words to say to me. It had been a few years since we had spoken. I told her about the Monet gardens and how I would have loved for her to see them, and I told her how I was planning to travel again.

She expressed excitement and joy for me, and she encouraged me to go on my trip to Ecuador.

ONE MORE LET-DOWN

My roommate Thad drove me to the airport for my departure. I had two layovers, one in Chicago and one in Miami. They were quick, but I didn't get to Quito until late at night. I was in a bit of a daze, and I didn't really know what to expect. My partner met me at the airport and we took a cab back to where she was staying. I took a shower, and we went to bed.

We explored as much of Ecuador together as we could in those few days, and in the middle of it, I got a phone call. My stepmother had passed away.

My father and I were both in shock that she went so fast, and I knew that my father was torn about this. He loved her. I was sad, but I also had emotions that no one could understand, except maybe those who grew up in the House of Yahweh. Death was a little different for us.

Even us "fall-aways". We knew how they viewed death. We also knew how sicknesses like these were taught to be the result of some sin that we committed. Death to us who had left was a dark thing. Those in the House of Yahweh were taught not how to grieve, if anything. All my father would speak of was the "resurrection", where he could see her again.

I left Quito and flew to Atlanta to see my cousin. It was short but sweet. We were able to connect in ways that we hadn't before. We were older now, and we had our lives more together. She'd been through a lot, and she was blossoming into a beautiful woman. The last day there, I emptied my checking account to pay a credit card bill online. The credit card itself was still in Michigan. This was a big mistake.

I got to the airport and I had a flight delay due to 'slight rain'. I was flying from Atlanta to Chicago, and I had another flight to catch. After a six-hour delay I missed my flight, and I had to spend the night in the airport. When I got to Chicago I learned that my next possible flight out was in two days.

"Two fucking days? Are you kidding me?" I thought while reminding myself that I had $4 in my checking account. I was stressed, stunned, and probably not seeing as clearly as I could've been.

I called my friends, and I called my brother. Thad offered to drive out. He said his brakes were bad but he would still make the run if I wanted. My brother told me to call Mom in the morning. "She's not really happy with you, being that you went on the trip to Ecuador, but I'm sure she'll help you out, get a warm meal in you, you know? She's only an hour away, just wait until the morning to call her. She's sleeping now."

"I don't know man," I said.

"She's your mother, dude."

A couple of ladies were sitting next to me as I had this conversation with my brother. When I hung up the phone, they came over with a bag filled with toiletries, a couple of energy bars, and a few extra dollars. "We heard your story, and we're really sorry. Hopefully this will help make things not so difficult."

172

"Thank you, that's very kind of you. I really appreciate it," I said.

"Just make sure you tell people if anyone asks that it was two nice ladies from Seattle who offered some help."

"Will do," I replied with a smile on my face.

I went to sleep and the few hours of loud lobby music passed too quickly. I was awakened by a security officer and told I needed to move. It was four in the morning, and I needed to wait a few hours before I called my mother.

I found some benches I could actually lay down on in the Canadian section of O'Hare. 6:30 a.m. rolled around, and then came the moment of truth.

I called my mother. On the other end of the phone I was greeted with, "Why are you calling me so early in the morning?"

I explained to her that I had waited 14 hours to call her, and that I knew she tended to get up early.

"Well what do you want?"

I explained my situation, and the tone in her voice got more aggressive. I don't remember her exact words, but a fight was coming. She wasn't going to do anything to help me, which I expected. Maybe I was only asking because a part of me wanted to tell my brother, "Yeah Erik, I called her and I already knew what the answer was."

I don't remember the exact exchange, but I didn't fight back. I was too tired. I did remind her that I hadn't asked her for anything since before I went to college.

I called my brother and told him what happened. He couldn't believe it. I called my housemate, who became furious. No one could believe what had happened. My mother was only an hour away from Chicago, and it was a weekend. There was nothing stopping her from coming to get me.

CANCER WASN'T HER FAULT

Back home, my friends picked me up from the airport and were sorry to hear about my stepmother. Regardless of everything, when we got to the pad and poured some drinks, my friends launched into a relentless dialogue about my situation with my mother at the airport. Loud shouts of disbelief at what a mother could do.

Looking back, I'm glad I had the support I did. I was learning that friends, too, can be family. Even though situations can seem incredibly difficult at times, things will work out. Maybe this is what my mother was trying to teach me, but at the time, I was only being taught who not to ask, and who to keep a distance from.

A few weeks after my return, I scheduled a time to meet up with my father at a coffee shop in Marquette. We hadn't sat down together for years, but now I felt empathy for him. But still, there were things that I needed to express to him, for both of our own good. I had expressed those feelings to my partner, and she did her best to understand, but I needed to tell him directly. We sat down at the table and I looked at him and said, "You know, I know Linda was begging for forgiveness before she died." I was interrupted by my father's uncontrollable tears.

He didn't know how I knew that. But I knew, because this was the dynamic of the cult.

"I felt really bad for her," I said.

"She prayed and cried every night asking for forgiveness." My dad said as he tried to hold in his tears.

"And she didn't need to. She did nothing wrong," I replied.

"I think she was taking too much colloidal silver. I found many empty bottles next to her bed. John Bragg's wife must have been telling her to take that."

I had no response to their superstitious cleanses. I felt sincere pain for my father and what Linda had gone through.

My father put his wife's body in a black body bag, tagged it with the proper licensing and drove her from Marquette, Michigan, to Clyde, Texas, to have her buried in the House of Yahweh cemetery. This is where Linda wanted to be buried. Later that summer, her sister would come and visit. It was a peaceful time, and it was nice to see her. She reminded me of Linda, as a sister should.

College graduation was rolling around, and I was excited to be done. I wasn't sure what I was going to do, but I knew I was leaving Marquette. I didn't know for how long, but I knew I was going and that I needed to go. My grades were good, and I'd even made it on the Dean's lists.

No one would've expected that, given my history in high school.

GRADUATION

As graduation came closer, I knew that I wouldn't be going to go to the ceremony. I didn't want to pay for the gown, and I didn't want to have to wake up early to hear Dr. Wong's cliche and repetitive speeches.

I know it sounds a bit cynical, but performing solo piano for student orientations proved to me that Wong had used the same speeches for years. They were what you'd expect from a politician.

The other main reason I chose not to go to graduation was because I didn't want my mother there. A part of me felt that, if she could so effortlessly refuse to help me with anything throughout college, then she shouldn't take part in the joy and pride of me finishing.

"She wasn't a part of any of it," I said to myself one day, exhaling cigarette smoke. I was getting a degree and that was good enough.

My aunt was kind enough to throw me a graduation party. The Salo side of my family definitely knows how to throw a party. My good friends were there, my partner was there, and my father was there. He was able to see who my friends were, and he could see who I had become at that point in my life. I was secure with who I was, and I was finally able to share at least a little love with him. I knew he was proud of me and glad that I'd figured out a way to make it on my own.

I was working as a technical writer before I graduated from university. A friend of mine through school helped me tailor my resume to get the job. It was convenient work, because it allowed me to work from anyplace I had internet. This is what I planned to do for a while, until I'd progressed with whatever my career would turn out to be.

Some days I wrote almost 10,000 words, but because it was often technical jargon, as far from art as one could get, I never considered myself a writer at that point.

My aunt and uncle invited me to stay with them before I moved to Colorado, so many mornings were spent on their couch in front of the television, socializing over coffee while I worked. It was nice to spend time with them before I left on a new journey.

I planned to go to Colorado for a while, then leave to Ecuador again, where I would live with my partner for a period. One of my college professors, a dear friend of mine, was planning on driving to California to visit her family. So on the way, she figured she could drop me off. And as a part of the deal, I could do most of the driving on the way there.

6. LEAVING MARQUETTE

The friend I was going to see in Colorado was a man who I'd worked with throughout college. We worked as maintenance men for a real estate company in Marquette. Our job could be anything from painting, to plastering, to ceiling tiles, to lawn maintenance, to using carpet extractors to suck up sewage from basements with low ceilings on hot summer days.

Dave was the type of guy that you might refer to as a "tough motherfucker". He didn't really look it from a distance, but one glance at his fighting Irish blue eyes, and you knew he was a fighter, just as much as he was a lover. Tall, slender, and darkened from the sun, and born in Detroit, just like my father. He had a few years on me, but that never stopped us from "shooting the shit" or shooting pool.

We were friends throughout college, and I never saw his dark side. Speaking of shooting pool, one night at a bar when I was 19, we were having drinks and cleaning up the house.

"Don't get too friendly with this guy, Brandon," Dave whispered in my ear. "He's a cop."

It was like he could smell cops from a mile away.

Dave graduated from university a couple of years before I did, with a 4.0 GPA, mind you. Again, from a distance, you only got a fuzzy color image of a thick book. He'd worked all over the United States. He'd been a sailor, mechanic, carpenter, chess player, reader, debater, geologist, and other things. When I was done with school, he invited me to stay with him for a few months out in Durango, and that was the plan. It was time to make some changes and have a change of scenery.

My professor, Jeanne, and I drove from Marquette to Durango. Along the way, while we were visiting her niece in Wisconsin, she got the wonderful news of becoming tenured at the university. She and all of her friends and family were thrilled. She was so thrilled, she treated us to Dom Perignon champagne, a decadent treat.

There wasn't one dull moment during that trip. Even on the drive from Madison to Boulder, which we did in one shot. A couple of days later we arrived in Durango at night. She was surprised how easy I took all the driving, but I reminded her of the 36 times I had driven all the way from Texas from Marquette. Arriving at my friend's house, they had some Chinese food ready to munch on, and beds prepared.

It sure was nice to see Dave. Jeanne had really sensitive allergies and was a little cautious about the cats and the free-roaming ferret, so she felt more comfortable getting a hotel room.

Durango was something new. A small town, and people were quite friendly. The first couple of weeks were spent writing technical articles at a coffee shop in the mornings. That was where I randomly ran into a guy, also named Brandon, who was working for the same company. The afternoons were spent helping Dave with some odd jobs, and then after work we went on hikes or played disc golf.

ODE TO MY SOCKS

One day in Durango, I was in a shoe store on Main Street. It was the nicest shoe store for miles, and I was only there to browse. After about 10 minutes, I realized that I was standing next to a cheerful man looking at the same shoes as I was.

"These are pretty nice shoes," I said to him.

"Yes indeed, if only it were as easy to find a nice pair of socks," he replied.

Having recently bought an extremely comfortable pair of socks made from bamboo, I told him all about them.

"What do you do?" he asked me, and I told him I was a technical writer.

"Well, I have a web design company right down the street. Why don't you come down around 5 p.m.? I might have a job for you."

I went to his office and met his work partner. He told me what they did, which was online business marketing, and he thought that I might be a good fit with his company for certain projects that he had going on. He wanted to test me by giving me the opportunity to build my own website. He set me up with my own domain, 'brandonsalo.com', and said, "Let's see what you can do by Monday."

After a weekend of partying, I woke up Monday morning having done nothing with the website, and I went to the coffee shop to do what I normally did. Then I remembered, and I started to work on the site. About 40 minutes later I made some changes, and updated some things, and I got a message from this guy Bill. "I like your site, why don't you come down to the office and start work today."

I showed up to the office, and he said, "You know, most people won't do anything with their site. The fact that you did says something." I was glad that I at least did something.

Bill at 'E7 Systems' introduced me to the real world of business. Being only 25, I was still young and naïve, and I still had a bit of an attitude about things. I thank my memory for learning from the lessons he taught me, all these years after the fact.

He had me work as a liaison between clients and programmers, and giving presentations to clients, and organizing information for the company. I owe much of my business knowledge to him and his company, and despite some moments of immaturity, his patience and my growth into adulthood have allowed us to continue a warm relationship.

It was a few weeks before I'd left that company to live in Ecuador that he helped me build the website 'cultsurvivor.com'. We had a long discussion over deciding the right name for it. This was when I first figured I was ready to start writing a book about growing up in a cult. The time wasn't quite right, yet, but if it wasn't for Bill, it probably wouldn't have been written the way it was.

INDEPENDENCE ABROAD

I have to say I owe it to my mother for teaching me to have an outgoing personality, friendly and charismatic. Without her, I probably wouldn't have been able to accomplish the things that I have, especially in terms of employment or public speaking. People seemed to like me, and the older I got, the more I began to see myself in a clearer light, and over time, this is perhaps what made people like me even more.

I purchased my ticket from Denver to Quito, exactly $613 for the round trip. This was going to be the "make it or break it" experience for my partner and me, and a good chance for me to see more of a different part of the globe, and a different part of myself.

My partner taught elementary students at one of the local schools, on a typical 8-to-4 schedule during the week. While she was at work, I would generally work from 8 a.m. to noon. After I was finished, I'd spend the rest of the working day exploring Quito. I would go to the local food markets, to buy food for dinner, play piano at the local restaurants and hotels, and make friends with locals. Quito was a different world for me. The people were kind and relaxed, much more so than I'd ever experienced in the United States. Also, Quito is at an altitude of 3,000 meters. The air felt thin, but the horizon gave a view to spectacular ice-capped mountains. There was something special about those mountains, and I liked the altitude. Something about it made me feel fresh, clean and clear-headed.

One night in Quito I went to a jam session where a trio was playing. A bass player, guitarist, and drummer were playing some standards at a place called El Libro. I tried to show the musicians that I was really paying attention, and once they'd recognized that, the guitarist called out 'Giant Steps' a Coltrane tune that's rather difficult to play. He counted the tempo so the half-note equaled 120 beats per minute. It was way too slow, and the last thing that I wanted to hear. Afterwards, a saxophone player told me that it's a really hard tune to play on the bass. I just looked at her, and she stopped talking. I walked out of the bar and then I met three people: a photographer, a sax player, and his wife. Three people who'd become dear friends of mine for the rest of my life.

The photographer was from Chicago, but born in Russia. The sax player, Alejo, and his wife Moni were both from Ecuador. From that time on, we'd meet often, and we spent countless hours playing music with each other. The photographer wasn't a musician, but a great appreciator, and he too would spend those countless hours with us. When we were together but not rehearsing, we'd be partying, and partying in Ecuador consists of everything you could imagine in South America.

That was most likely the tip of the wedge that drove my partner and me apart. She liked different aspects of the partying than I did. One night, I had to pick her limp body off the floor of a pub, panicking and fearing that she might never come back. A few slaps across her face and shouts in her ears brought no response. Without thinking, I looked around and grabbed a bottle of water from a table and threw it at her face. She came to, but she was in a daze.

Our usual friends weren't with us that night, but another good friend was. His nickname was 'The Fighter', a smart and easy going man who liked to party. He was also a musician, which is how our friendship started. He left the pub to get a cab. The pub owners were closing the place, so we had to wait outside.

Lo and behold, we found ourselves surrounded by thugs. Not a good situation when you're having to take care of a half-conscious gringa. 'The Fighter' returned with a taxi, and one of the thugs tried to steal my partner's purse. It was a poor attempt, and I'm glad they didn't succeed. Later that night, she told me the most heart-breaking words I'd ever heard from her: "Next time, I just won't do as much."

MAKING CHANGES

My partner and I had travelled through much of Ecuador. We'd seen most of the country together, and she was even there to hold my hand when I had amoebic dysentery and needed treatment in an emergency room. Living in Ecuador doesn't get more spectacular than that. I had fluids screaming out of both ends of my body. Intense stomach cramps, kidney pains from dehydration, and incredible fatigue.

The cab driver who took us from the apartment to the Hospital Metropolitano made haste in getting us there. Five hours later, I had received IV medication, blood test, stool test, and a comfortable rest in a hospital bed. I said to Athena, "Take a picture." She did, and shortly after, we could hear other camera shutters going off through the curtains of the beds next to us. The whole hospital visit came to $100. I couldn't believe it. Incredibly cheap, and I thought the care was excellent. After that visit, I was more or less bed-bound for a couple of weeks, with a special diet. Thankfully my job could be done from bed, and in those two weeks I accomplished a lot.

We travelled a little more before we left Ecuador. We visited the Amazon, and the cloud forests of Santa Lucia. By the time we left, our relationship had some serious wounds. We often fought in the mornings, and sometimes I had to dodge flying dishware. Her intentions were to go teach abroad again in another country, and I was going to go back to Michigan, to see my brother's second child.

Back to Marquette, I stayed with friends for a month. I was still writing, but there was a shift in the work flow, which started to decline. Soon I'd be looking for other work, and what I least expected was that finding decent work would be so difficult. Within a couple of months I was applying for work anywhere, for jobs that started at $8 or $10 an hour, but no one was hiring.

I had many published articles by that time. Good work experience, and a degree. However, I couldn't find anything worth staying in Michigan for. Eventually I got a job managing a liquor store for $7/hour. My boss and I had a fluctuating relationship. Sometimes we got along great, and sometimes he expressed that he was having a very bad day. The job was very depressing for me. My entire situation was depressing. In fact, I was more depressed about my life than I had ever been.

Thoughts of suicide came naturally to me at that point. I didn't talk to anyone about them, because I knew I wasn't going to act on them. But I knew I needed to make a change.

I was playing in a band that didn't seem to go anywhere. Often I was left confused, whether the lead singer was seeking what others in the band were seeking, or whether he was simply guided by his ego. If felt like a dead-end, just like my job dealing with the local alcoholics at 11:00 a.m. I felt pity for them, but there was nothing I could do.

One day at work I found myself looking out the liquor store window at my bicycle, and I thought to myself, "I'm going to ride my bike to Maine. I'm sure I can find at least another liquor store there to work at, and at least it will be a different scene." So that was my plan. I would ride my bike across the country to escape the dead-end mundanity that surrounded me. I needed to do something, I was in an incredibly dark place.

There was another side to my mental ailments, most likely provoked by another issue that I had going on. Shortly after returning to my hometown, I noticed that I had a cough and frequent bloody noses. Later those coughs turned into joint aches, and massive headaches. I had no idea what was going on. I was able to work out, but I had trouble gaining weight. I was also eating a lot.

About two weeks before departing on my bicycle trip, I passed what turned out to be a giant round-worm. I was horrified. "Thad!" I yelled, "What the fuck dude? Look what happened?"

Thad in his nonchalance said, "Yeah, it happens. It's not a big deal."

"Dude, don't tell anyone."

"I won't," he replied. It turns out that these things can live inside someone for years before they know. They only leave your body once they die. I most likely had hundreds of them inside me. I was disgusted.

Shortly after I accepted my condition, I was no longer shy about it, and found myself talking openly about it to anyone. This was one of the ways I got over things that were bothering me. I wasn't sure what to do, to get rid of it, because I didn't have the money to see a doctor. I spoke with a friend of mine who I'd met in Ecuador, and he told me to get Ivermectin. I did some research on the medication, and it seemed to be what I needed.

I searched the internet to find where I could buy this drug, and a pet store in Missouri had it for sale. They also sold syringes. I bought the medication and the syringes. I was determined to finish this mess. In the meantime, while waiting for the medication to arrive, I spoke with a friend of mine who was an MD. He said that I was right about the medication that I needed, but he wasn't sure about the medication I bought. He wrote me a prescription to pick up from Walgreens.

I cancelled my order and picked up the pills. "You must be a good host," the doctor told me.

I took the pills, and the next day everything seemed to have passed. From that moment on, there were no more headaches, joint pains, heart palpitations or hunger pains. Soon I would be on my bicycle to a different life.

PREPARING FOR THE JOURNEY

About one month after I'd decided to ride my bike to Maine, I thought that maybe I could try my luck in Montreal. It was on the way, since I was going through Canada. I figured that I could play piano there, and probably have good luck doing other types of work as well. Montreal seemed like a good bet. Plus, I had an interest in French, and maybe I could learn more of that, too.

I saved up about $400 for this trip. I didn't have a cell phone, but I had a folding keyboard that fit inside my B.O.B. bicycle trailer. With only $400, I knew I wouldn't have much money for food, so that's where my food stamps came in. Since I was making so little money to support myself, the government pitched in for my food. I saved up about 40 days worth the food for the trip.

Some of my friends thought I was crazy, and some thought it was really cool. My mother told me it was the stupidest idea I had ever had, but when she said that, it reminded me how I always felt she was resentful that I travelled in general.

My cousin asked me, "When are you coming back?"

I said, "Well I sure as hell ain't riding my bike back." He laughed.

The truth is, I didn't plan on coming back. I didn't know if I ever would. There wasn't anything in Marquette for me, and I knew I needed a long break from it, especially after clearing my head spending countless hours pedaling through the Canadian summer.

I left on June 13th. I planned for that date, because it's special to me. My father gave me a hug before I left, and he showed excitement, joy, and concern. We both had a bit of gloss in our eyes from that moment.

I asked Thad to drive me to Munising to get me started. I wanted it that way because I knew if I started a little farther out of town, I would be less likely to turn back. There was no turning back, and I needed to be sure of it. Thad's the type of person who would generally do anything for anyone, and he gladly gave me a ride. Hell, it's hard for him to get out of bed for work, but if a friend calls him at an even more inconvenient time, he's right there.

Thad dropped me off at a gas station and watched me set up my rig. I had four saddle bags, a tool bag, a hiking pack, and a trailer. It was three times the weight that any sane person would ever tour with. Thad wanted to give the bike a ride before I left, so I let him. He got a kick out of it. We hugged and parted ways.

I slowly took off and headed east down the road that the locals refer to as the Seney stretch. It would take me two days to ride 120 miles to Canada. Later that night I slept in my hammock off the side of the road, tucked away between two spruce trees. I cooked breakfast the next morning and continued heading east. I needed to make it to Sault St. Marie that day, a friend from my childhood was waiting for me. He was going to host me for a few nights before I continued into Canada.

ON A BICYCLE

17 miles from the end of the trip to Sault St. Marie, the word 'challenge' gained new meaning for me. The wind was coming at me forcefully, and I couldn't pedal myself faster than 4 miles per hour. I stopped to lay in the grass. The sun was receding, and I was overcome by dizziness. I had never been so exhausted before.

I got on my bike and I continued pedaling. Within a couple hours I made it to my destination. Dizzy, nauseous, and dramatically tired, I went to the bathroom only to see myself urinate a brown liquid that would normally bring me great anxiety. I had never seen such a thing before, but I was too tired to care. I needed to eat, but I wasn't even hungry.

We bought steaks that night, and it helped me regain my strength. Later that night, Isaac and I were on the town. He showed me his current stomping grounds. It felt great to catch up with him.

Couch-surfing was something I had planned on doing if I wasn't going to sleep in the woods, so the night after I left my friend's house, I would cycle from his town to Thessalon, Ontario, where I'd meet my first host. He had chickens, a cat, and a performing arts theatre. He was interested in doing a music project with me. Tom turned out to be a good friend who I would stay in contact with from then on. We shared a lot of the same values.

Later, I stayed with another host in Sudbury, who also became a good friend. I managed to get several piano gigs in Sudbury, and my finances stayed pretty even. My hosts even took me out to eat, here and there, which I hadn't expected at all. Shortly after being in Sudbury, I got a phone call from a girl who I'd been seeing before I left.

"I'm late," she said. "Very late."

I was nervous, and in shock. I believed her, because she wasn't lying, she was only being honest. I was sure that I would get to Montreal, only to pack my things and go back to start a family.

She had taken pregnancy tests, but they were inconclusive. My worst fear was to go back to a town that I had ended up despising, to settle down with a family that I wasn't ready to have. Also, having to further face the depression that put me on that bicycle in the first place.

I thought to myself, "Well at least it's with her."

I headed to North Bay, Ontario. I made it there in one day, and again I was exhausted.

I carried the weight of what might happen on my journey, and I tried to continue without letting it get to me too much. I just had to wait and see. After a few performances and an interview, I left for Ottawa. It was Canada Day, and on that day I got a phone call.

"I got my period, I'm not pregnant."

We were both happy. We were able to resume our intended paths.

A DARK REMINDER

Often, I would speak via Facebook to people who'd also left the House of Yahweh. It turned out that a lot of people had left since I did. There was a boy who cried when I left (or so my father told me), and it turned out that he had left has well. I couldn't believe how many people had left. I wasn't sure why, but my guess at the time was that it had kept changing for the worse.

I found Samantha on Facebook. I was so happy to see that she was gone! After being married to a man in his 70s for a few years, I could only imagine what she'd been through.

Around that time, Yisrayl Hawkins was being prosecuted for polygamy, and his bond was set at $10 million. One of the highest-ranking elders was also being prosecuted, for child molestation. Yedidyah Hawkins was said to have been checking his step-daughter's vagina with cotton swabs and medical equipment, to see whether she was still a virgin, or if she had cervical cancer. This was the tip of the ice-berg of the rumors spreading, but many were sure that he was guilty, and some people were kicked out of the House of Yahweh for testifying against Yedidyah.

"Yahweh will be the final judge," is what Yisrayl said, and anyone getting in the way of that would be guilty of great sin.

Yedidyah was put in prison for several years. Unfortunately, many who were still in the house of Yahweh believed that he shouldn't have gone to prison. Some of the

194

elders allegedly told him that he had every right to violate that young girl in such a way. Remember, women are owned by the men, who are the heads of their households.

In that light, it follows that women have no rights. They simply need to do as instructed. And the first and foremost rule of Yisrayl Hawkins is: "Don't question, and don't doubt the teachings."

Yisrayl Hawkins got off on all charges. His Lawyer, David Young, managed to get the bail reduced to something Yisrayl could throw cash at without looking suspicious. I saw Young's name in the news and I thought to myself, "Is he related to Gary Young? The guy that came to the cult to sell essential oils?" Because if that was the case, his company would have been part of the big picture for making a lot of money.

I heard some stories about Samantha. Not from her directly, but through word-of-mouth. Yisrayl Hawkins was said to have stored his semen in ice-trays, and kept it in the freezer. He would later use this for pregnancies, according to someone who knew one of his wives.

Hearing the news about Yedidyah and Yisrayl made me think of the time I saw Yisrayl on the 'Nancy Grace' show. He was asked question after question, and he lied about everything. Maybe lying for righteousness' sake was okay, and he was really good at it. People were allowed to call into the show and ask questions. I stood in front of the TV screen watching his lips as he said that scientists were doing research that paralleled prophecy from the Bible. My thumb kept hitting redial, so I could get through on the phone.

"What scientists?" Nancy wondered.

"I can't tell you what scientists, but I can tell you that they are," Yisrayl responded with a smirk on his face.

I tried to get through to talk to him directly, in public. I wasn't afraid to say that he was lying about everything. That he lied about his wives, and about the trained guards who watch and protect the House of Yahweh compound. He made up everything he was saying. Then lo and behold, a familiar voice comes over the speaker, on the air.

"Hi Yisrayl, can you tell me more about science and Bible prophecy."

Nancy's eyes rolled – it was David Heimerman, who'd got through with the phone call.

"Of course," Yisrayl said, going back to his sales pitch.

I saw a movie in my mind of several members from the House of Yahweh in Wisconsin, all trying to make the phone call, and when one got through, they would hand the phone over to David. In my mind, I could hear all the chants as David spoke to Yisrayl: "Praise Yahweh!"

I could hear their voices in my head.

From then. I started to wonder whether David himself was lost, or else in on the business plan himself. He had a degree in Engineering, so you might assume that he was pretty intelligent. It seemed unlikely that he'd found himself in a moment of desperation that led him to believe a lot of what Yisrayl had to say. Could Heimerman be profiting from this as well?

That was a question that I started to ask myself. If that were the case, it would make sense why he gave so much attention to my father about paying his tithes, giving free-will offerings, spending so much time working for free for the house of Yahweh, directly under his supervision.

WHAT A BICYCLE MIGHT BRING

I eventually made it to Montreal, just in time to blow some steam at a jam session in one of the Hyatt hotels. Two outstanding musicians from Boston shared the stage with me. After the first tune we played, the trumpet player ran up to me and said, "You want to play some blues? How about some blues in F?"

"Yeah."

"You start," he said. My left hand hit a F and a C in the bass of the Yamaha grand. I closed my eyes and laid down a groove with the bassist and the drummer. The horn players started to kill it. When it came time for my solo, I kept my eyes shut and played the way Dane and Alex taught me how to play, which was with all the heart I have.

Shortly into my solo I could hear the two horn players shouting, "Yeah! Yeah!!"

I couldn't tell you what either of my hands did. I just played as honestly as I could. And even though to some it seemed louder than other piano players, the two brothers from Boston appreciated it most, and that was all that mattered to me.

"Don't hold back. Ever." That was my lesson. And why should I? When it comes time to say something, we need to say it. If it's not time, then wait. The time will come.

Montreal treated me well. I worked as a jazz pianist, I played with many great musicians there. I played at McGill and the University of Montreal. I worked as a carpenter and a landscaper. I even fell in love with one of the kindest women I had ever met. She was the first person I had a relationship with who was truly passionate about something – cooking. And wow, could she cook! And to top it all off, her entire family was kind, and she came from a background that was much more stable than mine. I saw that as being very important, if she were someone who I'd be with for a long time.

One day, I left her house to head back to my apartment on my bicycle. I went to take a left turn and "Smash" – a car hits me. I had a split-second to accept what was going to happen. I saw the car, stood up, and let go of the handle bars to take the hit.

Sliding on to the windshield, I hit my head pretty hard. I continued over the top of the car and landed on my back. Of course it was the one rare time that I wasn't wearing a helmet. By the time I got home, I realized that I needed to go to the hospital. The guy who hit me had made a quick check to see if I was alive. I told him I was worried my teeth were gone. He wrote down a fake phone number and took off.

"You need an MRI, but it's going to cost $900," said the nurse in the emergency room.

"But my vital signs are okay, right?" I didn't want to pay the $900, because a week before that my $3000 keyboard had been stolen. So I neglected it and decided to tough out the next few days with some rest. That night, Katheryn woke me up every couple of hours to make sure I was okay.

As special and as kind as she was, she wasn't able to undo the knots that life had tightened for me. Not that I was thinking she had to – subconsciously I thought that maybe they would be undone naturally, just being with her, but I was wrong. I needed to part ways again with a person who I would always care about.

I wished that things could've been simpler. I wished I hadn't done that to her. Despite the fact that the relationship came to an end, her kindness made the breakup as easy as it could be. She was truly a great person.

She encouraged me to write my story, and I tried. But at that point, I wasn't able to stay with it. She and her entire family encouraged me to write it down, and if it wasn't for their encouragement, I might have never done it.

Toward the end of my stay in Montreal, I decided I would work on a TEFL certificate to teach English abroad. I created the idea that maybe I could find a job I could tolerate while I travelled. I figured I could save money over a few years, to eventually invest in some property in Ecuador. I've always thought it would be nice to retire there.

As my departure from Montreal grew closer, a friend of mine who ran a foundation in Ecuador offered me work down there. He said he would fly me down if I worked for his foundation, but that he needed me there now. I had originally wanted to leave toward the end of summer, but I figured, "why not." I packed up my things and left.

I had been getting worn out with my work situations. The longer I stayed at both of my jobs, the more I felt taken advantage of. It wasn't worth it to continue.

I was picked up by someone who worked for the foundation in Rousse's Point, and we headed to Albany,

New York, where the headquarters were located. On the way there, the car broke down, and we needed to get a tow. This was where things got weird.

The owner of the car, Greg, had AAA insurance. However, he was never in the country to use it, and at that point he was in India, so he told me to pretend that I was him, so he wouldn't have to pay the cost for the tow. I went along with it. When it worked out, he called back to apologize, and he gave what seemed to be a sincere apology. Later that night, his worker and I arrived at the house that was their headquarters. This was where I started to see that everything was very unorganized.

I went to sleep and woke up the next day, ready to start helping with the work. Things needed to be more organized, so that's what I helped to do. A couple days passed, and it was found out by Greg that I had two cans of beer in the fridge. I wasn't aware that this was a big 'no-no' and I was on the verge of being kicked out of the foundation. I was furious. I couldn't believe that something so simple would put me on the streets. Because of that, my skepticism started to grow.

I found a local bar down the street that had a piano. I'd go there every night while in Albany to play for tips and soup before I left for Ecuador. One night, after four hours of playing, several rounds of applause, and $4 in tips, I was a bit annoyed. A dark gentleman and his lover asked me to play for them, so I did. They enjoyed it and offered to take me out for drinks and dancing. This seemed to be exactly what I needed. Just to let loose.

CHANGE OF PLANS

Later that night we danced to Latin music, just the three of us, and it was great. Off in a dark corner I noticed a woman who was dancing alone. I said to myself, "She seems like a groovy chick."

I walked over to see if she wanted to dance, and she put me off. I figured that was okay. So I went on and had a good time.

Eventually, I went outside to get some fresh air, and soon the three of us would be off to another bar. The woman in her flowered dress and jean jacket came running out. It appeared she wanted to talk to me. And so we did. We started talking, and soon we became interested in each other. That night was maybe the most romantic night I'd ever had in my life. I wasn't looking for it (consciously, anyway), and I knew that it was something I couldn't turn my back on.

She was leaving the next morning to meet her sister in New York City. She wouldn't be back for a week, and in a week was also when I was supposed to fly out to Ecuador. I delayed my flight by another week so I could spend time with her.

I was skeptical about the foundation, but I felt that I needed to go down anyway. I needed to learn more about the foundation, and say 'hello' and 'goodbye' to some dear friends. The woman and I spent a week together. We visited with her sister and friends, and we soaked up the summer sun of Albany, New York.

I arrived in Quito at night. At the layover in Bogota, I had met a Korean guy, and we'd decided to team up and grab a cab together. A cab is much quicker than the bus, and not so expensive when the cost is split between people. At the airport, I saw a couple who also appeared to be American or Canadian. Mind you, although there's only 40 million Canadians, it's more likely to run into them than Americans abroad. It turned out that they had a hostel booked. I told them it would be more convenient and quicker to get to the hostel if we all shared a cab, and that the Korean guy and I could stay at the same hostel if there was a vacancy. They agreed and it cost us $5 a piece for a 45-minute cab ride, so it worked out very well.

The next day I walked around and ate some of my favorite Ecuadorian foods. I tried to get in contact with Greg, but he was always hard to get ahold of. When he did respond, he just said, "Get on a bus to Tosagua, they're waiting for you. It's a small village. They know you're coming."

He expected me to go there with no contacts, no phone number, and just to be relaxed about it. He made it seem like it was a town of 400 people, when in fact it was a city of 40,000. When I brought this up later, he handed me a census from 2008. "Here, it's 30,000 people, see?"

Eventually I found the right bus to get there. My transfer involved a 200-yard hike through a field at 2:00 a.m. It was pitch black, and I could barely see the lights of the bus station that I was heading toward. No one spoke English, but that was okay.

I found the bus headed to Tosagua, and I hopped on. I asked the guy how far it was, and he said 15 minutes. I sat back and relaxed. 15 minutes later. I asked if we were there yet, and he said we had passed it. I recognized the town – I had been through there before, and he didn't even stop. He handed me 50 cents to catch the next bus back.

I arrived in Tosagua about 8:00 a.m. I asked several people if they knew about the foundation, but no one knew anything. "Of course not," I thought to myself.

An hour and a half later I was picked up by a motorcycle taxi and taken to my host family's house. I unpacked a few of my things and I went and checked out the church where I would be working.

Everything seemed okay until I started to realize what these people were being paid, and how they were being paid. As time went on, I became more and more aggravated. It seemed that for every dollar these people were getting paid, $50 was going to the foundation. And even though I was part of that foundation, I wasn't getting paid. No one was getting paid, except for the "accountant," who was the guy running the foundation.

Shortly after, I realized that I was coming down with a stomach infection. I started to take some Cipro, and I scheduled a doctor's appointment the next day. I always buy Cipro when I get to Quito, just in case.

When I got to the doctor's office, I was examined and told that I had to be tested for Dengue Fever. Little did I know that I was in a dengue epidemic area. I'd had no warning and was given no precautions to take. I figured that sleeping under a mosquito net was more for comfort, and not for safety.

While waiting for the blood test results, I was told to rest and drink a lot of fluids. Not to drink any alcohol or take Ibuprofen, only acetaminophen. The time came to get my results. I woke up from a nap and realized that no one was there. I went to leave the house and found that I was locked inside by a padlock. "What the hell?"

I had two options – pick the lock or climb an 8-foot picket bamboo fence. Thankfully I was able to find a smaller padlock that was easy to pick. Perhaps spending a little time with mischief in childhood can pay off later in life.

I was a little perturbed that I had been locked inside alone like that. It turned out that I did have dengue, plus a stomach infection. The fatigue, joint pains, and headaches increased as time went on, and it took almost a month for everything to heal properly.

The more time I spent working with the locals, trying to organize their work, the more frustrated I became. I couldn't stand the fact that they were being taken advantage of. I was working for free, but that was agreed. This was simply a case of someone who was business savvy, taking advantage of people who weren't so fortunate.

I couldn't blame the locals for not having access to decent education. I knew I was sharper than them, thanks to schooling and broad experience. But I also have ethics. I tried to explain the situation to them as tactfully as I could. I think they got something of an understanding. But Greg is very charismatic, and so they buy into that.

I left Tosagua and stayed with friends who had invited me into their home. They were always calm and kind, and it was quite a treat to share meals with them. A couple days after arriving at their place, I was out walking their dog. As we were about to cross a busy street, I ran with the dog, and it ran around and wrapped the leash around my legs. Face first, my forehead and mouth slammed into the curb.

I stood up and looked to my friend – "Mis dientes!" I pointed to my teeth. I thought they were gone.

"No, todo bien," he said. I was okay. But then he pointed to my forehead as I felt the blood rush down my face.

I pulled some tissue paper out of my pocket and waited for traffic to clear. It looked a lot worse than it was, but I needed to get a few stitches. I never have worries about visiting hospitals in foreign countries. Even in a town like Tosagua, where the cost is $5 and there's a horse tied up outside the entrance.

VENTURING BACK

I was planning on heading back to N.Y. I wanted to see the lady from Albany again. I knew that if I didn't, I would regret it for the rest of my life. I also knew that it would be complicated to separate myself from the foundation, being that they were my only source of work and housing. Plus, all of my things were there.

I felt confident that I'd be able to find work in Albany. I figure that if it was so easy in Montreal to get work under the table, then it should be even easier finding legal work in Albany.

I started looking for work as a carpenter. I had enough experience in the trades to do that, and in the meantime I could also look for professional work using my degree and other experience.

I left my friend's house in Quito and toured Ecuador for a while. I met up with a Brit named Dave. He and I became pretty good friends. We travelled to the coast together, and that was quite an adventure. We decided to take what seemed to be a short detour, to see some waterfalls, and it turned out to be an extra day but worth the bus rides to eventually make it to Puerto Lopez, where we would see the whales.

After seeing the waterfalls, we transferred buses a few times. Our last bus dropped us off in a very small town, and while they were letting us out, they pointed to a truck and told us to run to it and get in. So we did. We spent the last hour of our trip riding in the back of a truck to get to our destination, driving through the cold foggy backroads of west Ecuador.

More days of sight-seeing and nights of booze and laughter were our memories of Puerto Lopez. Dave was heading back to Quito, and I was heading to Montanita, a tourist town where I had planned on surfing. I said goodbye and I was on my way.

I arrived in Montanita and met up with an American who was studying there, before he went off to grad school. I took it easy that night. The next day, I had planned on spending the morning surfing, and then I'd hop on a bus to Guayaquil, where I would fly to Lima. I had a layover in Lima before flying back to N.Y.

While trying to surf at Montanita, I was lying flat on the board and the waves came and threw me off. I landed on the board sideways, and it pushed a couple of my lower ribs inward. It hurt quite a bit. I figured, maybe it's not that bad. I tried to get on the board again, and the pain was excruciating.

"Nope, that's it," I said to myself. These ribs were either broken or severely bruised.

Later that night, I would sleep on an airport bench before my flight left for Lima. I was uncomfortable to say the least. I bought an alarm clock to make sure I wouldn't miss my flight. Missing my flight would be the last thing my girlfriend would want to hear. I got to Lima, met up with a French couple, and soon we were off to try and find the cheapest cab we could.

I might advise that it's not always good being cheap in

unfamiliar countries. We found a cab that offered a low price, but when he told us where his car was, I started to get a little skeptical. We walked up to his cab, and I proceeded to get in the front seat.

"No, get in back," he said. This is when I knew something wasn't right. He then said that he was picking up a friend before he dropped us off. I hesitated, but I still got in the back with the French couple. I started to prepare for the worst-case scenario. Shortly after I closed the door, and before he took off, we were surrounded by cop cars.

They took us out of the cab and arrested the guy who was trying to take us. "He was going to rob or kidnap you," the police told us.

After that incident, we went with the first cab driver and headed to the center of Lima. "There's always some sort of rush in South America," I said to myself.

After a day packed with sight-seeing, I was off to New York. Two zopiclones, a couple glasses of merlot, and I was out like a light. I woke up and took a series of trains and buses to my stop at 34th and Broadway, and a $10 bus ride back to Albany. I couldn't beat it.

UNEXPECTED DIFFICULTIES

Still somewhat fatigued from the dengue fever, and sensitive thanks to my broken ribs, adjusting to a new life in Albany wasn't as easy as I'd hoped. I was starting new again, with $200, just like I did in Montreal. At least this time I had carpentry tools.

I looked for work and eventually found something that paid $15 an hour. Brad was the name of the contractor I worked for – me and two other guys worked under him. He told me stories of other guys who'd been hired and fired by him in the past, but that these days, times were good. He asked me if I had any injuries and I said no. Of course, I had to lie.

I worked pretty hard for this guy, and things were seeming to go well. Then one morning he came in looking more hung-over than usual and fired me out of the blue. I was devastated. There was no reason given, and even the other carpenter couldn't believe it. The other carpenter insisted that it was because the other guy kept calling in, and that it's what was making the boss angry. However, it's always easier to let the new guy go. I took it pretty hard. It had taken me a few weeks to find this job, and all of a sudden it was done, just like that.

The next day, I got a phone call from a wine store that I'd applied to. They wanted to hire me. They didn't offer many hours, but it was just enough to get by. I would be making about $90 a week. I'm not sure how I was able to stretch the money that far, but I somehow made it work.

I liked it there. The people were nice, and it gave me an opportunity to meet people in the community.

A week after I started working at the wine store in downtown Albany, Brad called me and asked how I was doing. He asked me if I wanted to do some drywall work for him. Not having much pride to swallow, I said yes, thinking I could really use the money.

I went back to work for him while working at the wine store. After a few days of just him and me working together, I began to get very tired of him bashing his two other workers.

"What kind of boss complains all the time about his employees? Especially when they're reasonable people?"

I was done. I looked down at him from the stepladder holding a paintbrush in my hand and said, "Brad, is it possible to get paid today, in cash?"

His eyebrows lowered and his voice quieted. "Yeah."

"Thank you," I said, and I went back to work. At the end of the day he handed me my money and I walked away.

"I'll call you later," he said.

I didn't respond, and he never called.

I felt valued at the wine store, and I was content with that for the time being. The owner, Mark, was leaving town for an uncertain amount of time to travel to Italy. During that time, the stock-boy stopped showing up to work. I could use the hours, so I picked up the slack.

While stocking the wine, I took it upon myself to make a big change in the storage room. I organized the pallets and made it a lot easier to unload our shipments. All of my coworkers were pleased and said it really needed doing. I was the youngest and strongest guy there, so why not?

I wasn't looking for a raise or for praise, I just wanted to show that I liked where I was working. How better to do it with than with a lot of sweat?

After a few weeks, Mark returned, and he was not happy. He was in the worst mood I'd ever seen. It turned out that the man he'd left in charge, called Bill, hadn't gone through with orders like he should have, and because of that, we were behind on stock.

Mark took me down to the storage room and yelled, "It should not look this empty."

I got angry. I'd been at the store for just a couple of weeks, and I had busted my ass just to put a smile on his face, and now I was baffled for being chastised. I had to hurry bringing boxes of wine up from the basement, and other boxes of wine back down. In the mix of things, I learned that a bottle of booze had been stolen, a very expensive bottle.

I was also told that it was me who had bumped a stool that touched a cord and knocked out a security camera. "I didn't put the stool there, Bill did."

But that didn't matter. "Who moved the bottle to the counter? It shouldn't have been moved there."

They spent time reviewing the cameras. "Who moved the bottle?" I asked.

"Bill did," Mark said.

The wine store was Bill's retirement job. Mark liked him and wouldn't question him about anything. I didn't get it.

Bill was 'conservative', not shy about his Tea Party views, while Mark had a dainty personality with a slight lisp in his phrasing. These two people are the types that you wouldn't think would mesh well.

So Bill had moved the bottle of booze, Bill put the stool where it shouldn't have been. When the camera was knocked out, I asked Bill about it, and he said, "I don't know anything about that, you'll have to wait for Mark to get back." Later that weekend, Bill threw a party at his house.

As I kept working on the day that Mark got back, I slammed my head against a rafter. I was full of outrage and ready to cuss out Mark for treating me like he had been. I walked upstairs and I said, "Mark, I hit my head, and I need to go home."

"Okay," he said.

The next day, I called a few hours before my shift and left a message saying that my head was still hurting, and I needed to rest. I also sent a text saying the same thing. He messaged me back saying that things weren't working out, and that I should let him know if I changed my address, in case the police wanted to talk to me about the stolen bottle of booze.

This was my second job in Albany. As if I would risk the only form of income I had, and desperately needed, for a bottle of booze.

7. NEW CONNECTIONS

In the meantime, I was enrolled in an EMT course. I had classes twice a week and made some new friends. I got a few piano gigs at one of the fanciest venues in Albany, which had $14 beers, plenty of scotches, and one of the most beat-up pianos I'd ever seen. The guy in charge of booking the gigs made things messy as well.

Dylan was the guy I was supposed to contact to book gigs. At first he seemed very helpful. He told me he always ran late on booking musicians, and that I needed to contact him toward the end of the month before I wanted to play. After weeks of trying to work with him, I had a conversation with the bar manager at Speakeasy.

"Dylan is really good at booking gigs months in advance."

"Really?" I didn't take it any further. I bit my tongue and just accepted the fact that I was being lied to, and led on, for months on end. My view of Albany really started to dim.

"Where am I?" I asked myself. "Is it me?"

Albany was difficult, and the only thing I had going for me was the EMT course. I posted an ad on Craigslist to offer my services as a pianist, and I got a few replies. The first was from this guy named James Kirk. It never dawned on me who else had that name. James was a bass player, and we got along very well. We became friends and ended up playing a few shows together.

Another response was from a guy named Jim Kelly. He wanted to build a band with his friends, and they wanted a keyboard player. Working with Jim and his band turned out to be one of the best decisions of my life. I didn't have a huge interest in the music they played – I was concerned with getting gigs to make my living. At the time, my grocery bill was $30 a week.

I shopped at a local Dominican store on Morton Ave, where Stefon Harris, one of my jazz idols, grew up. To pay my rent I was buying low on Craigslist and selling high on Ebay. I was somehow managing to get by like this.

The Jim Kelly band gave me a few gigs here and there, but more valuable was the friendship we created. The bass player, Mike, and his cousin John did me many favors as we got to know each other. John and Mike were always giving me rides to rehearsals, sharing drinks and smokes, and making me feel like a friend. John was a little skeptical of me at first, but who could blame him? I kept to myself at first, too.

BRIGHTER TIMES

December rolled around and James and I had a gig playing for the first female Mayor of Albany, at the University Club. My friends Jim and Gordon organized the gig. Mark from the wine shop was doing a tasting across the room for the same event. I must admit, my chest swelled with confidence when I learned I'd be performing in front of him the entire night. If it weren't for my musical training from Dane and Alex, I wouldn't be able to play with such confidence. I knew I would sound good, and playing with James, we'd only make each other sound good. We had a ball that night and received the nicest of compliments and applauses. Finally, I could see in Mark's eyes that he felt bad about what happened between us. He knew he was in the wrong, apologized, and we shook hands over it.

My gigs were few, whether with James or the Jim Kelly band. There seemed to be a lockdown on the available gigs in that small city. I got used to it. It wasn't about how good you were, or how versatile you were, but rather who you knew and who liked you. And from my experience as being the new guy so often, when you're new, you don't know many people; and when you meet people in the same field, they might not like you.

February was rolling around and I had promised my friend Sean down in Florida that I would participate in his wedding. I had no idea if I could afford it or not.

My relationship with Lucila had been on thin ice since November. She didn't want me to go, because she also knew

I probably couldn't afford it. But I never make promises without the intention of keeping them, which is why I rarely make them. I had to go.

After selling a few things on Ebay, I made barely enough money for the trip. The day before I left, I had two interviews: one at the state tax office, and another at a local bike shop. I told the employer at the bike shop that I was confident in getting hired full-time at the tax office, but that I still wanted the bike job, regardless. I knew that if I hadn't gotten those jobs, I'd be coming back to Albany from Florida only to pack my life onto a bicycle to try again somewhere else.

While down in Florida I received an e-mail from Dave, the owner of the bike shop. He wanted to hire me, so great – that was a start. Seeing my good friend in Florida so happy with his beautiful bride made me feel happy as well.

Back when I left Montreal, I had planned on flying to Florida from Ecuador, then going to South Korea to teach English. It's funny how things sometimes work out. I have to admit, staying positive with the circumstances in Albany seemed impossible at times. I was tired of just barely getting by, and I was tired of being in a relationship that was constantly struggling. I wondered if my entire life would always be one of struggle.

EFFORT FOR BENEVOLENCE

I started working at the bike shop shortly after returning. It was an hour-long bus ride from my house. I couldn't ride my bike in winter, but summer would soon come and I'd be able to get there faster. After a couple of weeks working there, I got a call from the tax office and they too wanted to hire me. I was excited. This would be my first job that offered health benefits.

I had applied to the local ambulance companies in January that year, right after receiving my EMT card. I didn't get a call from them until after a couple of months working at the tax office. They wanted me to come in for an interview around 4:00 p.m., and I told them I couldn't do it.

"Well it says on your application that you have full availability," the girl said over the phone.

"Yeah I did. Four months ago when I submitted it. But if I waited that long for you to call I would've starved to death by now." Something about that really annoyed me, especially since they were offering the same pay as the bike shop.

The next few months were spent working at the tax office. There were a couple of shops in the building that sold everything you'd find at a gas station. None of the food was healthy; the most consumed items were energy drinks and candy. Thousands of people worked on this campus, and being constantly surrounded by people who weren't encouraged to live healthy lifestyles was deeply depressing.

I'd leave work a little angry, often. If I saw candy, my stomach would turn. I felt that the tax office was draining me. I liked the pay, I liked the benefits, but it caused more stress than I felt was necessary.

After I started to get the hang of things, I began listening to lectures on Buddhism in the background while I did my work. If I couldn't have conversations of substance with those around me, then I would seek it on my own. I found Herbie Hancock's lectures that he gave at Harvard. I listened to those lectures over and over again. I thought they were beautiful, and perhaps the most beneficial words I could hear at that time. Soon I'd be meditating on concepts of compassion, uncertainty, acceptance. My path was starting to become clear.

I had been at the tax office for four months, and summer had set in. A couple days after a team meeting, at which we were told there had been no talks of lay-offs, we were laid off. They laid off 500 people, and that was that.

I was warned by my girlfriend that she couldn't handle me getting upset all over again, but I knew I wouldn't be able to help it. It was what it was.

A NEW BEGINNING

I still had the job at the bike shop, and that was great. I never really felt like my job was 'on the line', but who knows? I always kind of felt that things could change suddenly. I knew I wasn't needed anywhere, wherever I worked. But I did my best and kept on being a good worker, hoping that Dave at the bike shop was different. Shortly after being let go from the tax office, I got a little raise and more hours. I felt happy, and grew to trust Dave. I felt that things were stable there, and that he really was reasonable, which was new to me. I had never had as reasonable an employer as Dave.

As the summer dragged on, the relationship with my girlfriend grew thinner. My partner and I managed to get a car together, and that helped me pick up an extra carpentry gig down in Pennsylvania. We had moved in together a few weeks before I got laid off by the state. I spent a week down in PA, and that seemed to give the relationship a bit of breathing room, but it wasn't enough. Many things were pulling us apart. Maybe we just had different paths. I think in most breakups, where no one does any particular thing wrong, no one is really to blame. It doesn't take away from the sadness, but in this type of ending, no one is at fault.

Later that summer, my friend James from my jazz gigs told me that his company needed a new driver, and that since I had a car, I might be a good candidate for the job. I would need to get a business license, up my insurance, and do a few other things before I got started. I'd be making twice as much money as I had at the tax office, and I'd essentially be my own boss. It sounded like a good deal.

In the meantime, I was visiting Mike Coleman. I was familiar with his house by then because the Jim Kelly Band would rehearse there. He had a few projects that he needed help with, and since I wasn't an idiot with a tape measure or paintbrush, he could use an extra hand. He was never shy about buying drinks or dinner, always a great treat. Many times he would invite me over just to visit, and he even offered me money. I always refused the money, but I was glad he was offering help.

"Why don't you move in with me? I have an empty nest and the kids are gone. I'm going to be heating the place anyway," he said one day over a pint. I thought about it, and it seemed too good to be true. He had known me for a year at that point, and he'd seen everything that I had gone through. He felt I needed a break. My relationship with Lucila was nearing an end, and we needed to be apart anyway. I took him up on his offer.

When I met Lucila, I said to myself, if I don't try this out, I'll regret it for the rest of my life. And after everything that happened, I still wouldn't take back a minute of it. So I can say I have no regrets.

"You know why you don't fuck with an old man, Brandon?"

"Why?"

"Because he'll kill you." Mike said this as he stood in the kitchen. It didn't take me more than a minute to understand that this man was showing me sincere trust and love.

A NEW PERSPECTIVE

One night, Mike sat me down with his wife to discuss the terms of me staying there.

"Brandon's going to be staying here for an undetermined amount of time. He won't be here forever, but we're giving him a break for a bit to help him out," Mike said. Peri responded with "You're not much older than our children, so don't be surprised if we treat you like them. And please let us know if you're not coming home at night, so we don't worry about you." I smiled in reply. The truth is, I didn't know what a treat I was in for.

Shortly after moving in, I got settled into a routine. I was working as a courier during the week, and then on the weekends I was working at the bike shop. Mornings were spent at the gym and evenings were spent visiting with my new family. Sharing meals almost every evening was a warming feeling. Even the playful bickering that takes place between any couple who've loved each other for decades made me feel at home. And one evening, their daughter looked at me over the dinner table during a pause and said, "I think since you've been here, my parents fight less."

There were mornings where I had a lot of free time, and sometimes Mike would need an extra hand with some odd jobs. I was more than willing to jump on anything he asked me to do, and after some of these jobs he wanted to pay me. I always had to refuse. I simply couldn't believe his generosity. It's not like he didn't know what a help he already was to me; he was simply sharing what he could. His example of compassion began to seep into my being, and it pushed me further along a path that I was already on.

During my long drives from Albany to Utica and back, I had many hours to think about everything in my life. For the first time in life, my living circumstances provided me not only with financial stability, but emotional freedom and acceptance. By this I mean all of my expressed feelings were accepted as valid, and never once was I questioned about anything, ever. Nor did I ever feel that someone was questioning me in their minds. The feeling was completely surreal to me. It still is.

On those long drives I listened to recordings of TED talks, lectures on Buddhism, and endless recordings of Herbie Hancock, Donald Byrd, and many other great jazz artists. I began to feel centered in my being. I felt comfortable with who I was. I worried less, and I began to understand the value of family; and that gave me a growing sense of compassion for all those around me. It taught me meta-cognition, and how to guide my actions toward what I can prudently decide is right for me.

As autumn rolled in, I decided that my circumstances had provided a great opportunity for me to pick up on my old plans and go teach English in South Korea. For that, I needed to get some paperwork together, and the easiest way to get one of those documents was to go back to Marquette and get an 'Apostille' diploma. I scheduled time off from work and wondered if my Honda Civic with 240,000 miles on it would make the 2,000 mile round-trip.

The night that I left, Peri packed me a lunch bag with

sandwiches and snacks. I was off on the road. Thinking I could make it quite a ways without sleeping, I had to pull over at a rest area and sleep after the first 250 miles. Eventually I made it to the U.P.

I would be staying at my aunt and uncle's house for the time being, and to my surprise, my father was temporarily staying there as well. I hadn't seen him since the day I left for Montreal.

It was nice seeing my father. He was a little quiet and stoic, like the typical Finnish man. His skin looked healthy, and he looked good in general. But as always, his topics of discussion always tended to revolve around health cleanses and dietary supplements – more or less propaganda from the House of Yahweh. Backing his claims on doing liver cleanses continuously were books written in the 1920s. If the house of Yahweh told him it was science, he believed it. There was honestly no logic to many of his statements. I had known that for many years, but what I started to realize the last time I saw him broke my heart. I felt like the religion to which he had dedicated the past 25 years of his life had rotted his brain.

"The other day I was adding 6 and 9 and I wrote down 13. That's not the sum when you add 6 and 9," my father said as we were driving to my grandmother's house.
I couldn't believe his words. It seemed like a simple mistake anyone could make, but his words paralleled too many previous thoughts and feelings that I'd already had about him. I started to see an image in my mind, that certain parts of his brain were neurologically cut off, due to not being

used over the past couple of decades. I'm not a neuroscientist, or even a psychologist, but it made perfect sense to me, that if someone forces themselves to think in a particular way, eventually they won't be able to see things any other way.

I remember another conversation with my father: "I've spent 25 years already in the House of Yahweh, why give up now?"

During those moments, I still loved my father, and I showed him so, the best way I could. We had some moments of laughter, but there was also a time when I expressed something to him that I needed to get off my chest, and it needed to happen in front of everyone in the family. It took him by surprise, but I needed to say it out loud. I had just poured myself a small glass of scotch after getting out of the sauna. I sat down in the living room across from my father. We started to talk about Linda.

I looked him right in the eye and said, "Remember how I told you that I knew Linda was begging for forgiveness before she died? How she stayed up praying for forgiveness?"

"Yes," he replied softly.

"That's fucking bullshit dad. No one should have to do that, and she didn't need to be forgiven for anything. And that's one thing that's wrong about the House of Yahweh – for that environment to make her feel those things, right before she died."

My father turned his head and chin up and looked to his left with his eyes wide open. He tried to hold back his tears, but his eyes still watered up. My aunt, uncle and cousin sat in silence, but they knew that I was right in saying that to him. We all knew it wasn't to hurt him, but only to hopefully make him see – that a most unfair thing had happened to a lady that he truly loved.

My father had made the plans to move to Texas, which is why he was staying at his sister's house in the first place. When I first learned that he was sure he was moving to Texas, I was in New York. I was worried, because I thought that I might never see him again once he moved.

I wasn't the only person in the family who felt like this, either. We all were worried about him moving down there, and we all had the same fear: that we might never see him again.

When I left for New York, my father gave me the strongest hug he ever had. His left hand was clenched on my upper back, and his right hand was clenched on my lower back with the right side of his head pressed against mine.

"I love you," he said.

"I love you too, Dad," I replied.

I was back on the road, headed back to Albany. I had touched base with some good friends and mentors while in Michigan. "This guy left on a bicycle, and he came back in a car," was a quote that had made me feel good.

On the drive back, I was anticipating the drama that would take place between my mother and myself. She had found out through the grapevine that I'd visited the Upper Peninsula, but that I didn't drive another five hours further to see her. I could only think to myself, if she'd really wanted to see me, all these years, she would have bought me a bus ticket when I had the time and no money to do anything.

"I really want to see you, do you want to see me?" she asked.

"Yes." I replied.

"If you had a bus ticket to come see me, would you come and visit me?" she asked.

"Yes, mother."

"Well I'll have to think about that then," she said back in June, when I was so low in New York. She never called back after that, until I had returned to New York from my trip. The last thing I wanted was to argue with my mother, so I put off the conversation for as long as I could. I was glad to get back to my host family, and back to my routine. The thing is, at that house, no matter how bad of a day you might have had, the moment you walked through that main door, you felt good.

"Welcome back!" I was greeted with hugs and great company. I was so happy to be back.

Eventually I had to speak with my mother about the trip, and she did try to make me feel bad about not taking an extra day off to go and see her in Milwaukee. The truth is, I hadn't had the time to drive there. My schedule was tight as it was. She said that I was able to visit my father and not her, which made her feel bad. I said that I wasn't there for him, and it wasn't a lie. She said that I visited my sister and not her, and I said it was because it was on the way.

Then I told her I thought she was going to help me with a bus ticket back in June, and she told me that she didn't because I never called her back to ask for it.

I don't mean to batter my mother, because around this time I had started to learn about her illnesses; illnesses she never spoke to me about. I wasn't aware of all the medications she was on. I wasn't aware that she was bipolar. I knew she had a lot of serious struggles, but now I started to get a clearer picture of things.

I was finally able not to be angry with her about her actions, current or past. I started to accept them as completely beyond her control. Through that perspective, I started to discover a new type of love for her.

Despite the fact that I could view our relationship in a new light, the conversations with her were still emotionally exhausting. It was around Thanksgiving of 2014 that my siblings, my mother, and her new husband engaged in new drama. I was driving back to Albany from Utica during the largest snowstorm of the year. There was nearly a foot of snow on the highway, and the occasional car that would wiz by, fishtailing off in the distance. Some of these cars ended their journey in the ditch. I maintained a safer speed with my hands clenched around the steering wheel. I quickly glanced down at my white knuckles when my phone rang. I answered it on my headset. It was my sister.

"Moms in the hospital. She can't talk, and her husband John had to carry her into the ER," my sister told me frantically. "I'm really worried, and I feel guilty for not being there." My mother had fallen into some form of paralysis.

The doctors gave her two MRI's and a CAT scan. They couldn't tell what was wrong.

I engaged in an hour-long conversation with her husband. He insisted on me telling him what my mother did to her children that was so bad. Without going into detail, I only spoke of ambiguities and tried to express how being an honest person was one of the few important things in life. He told me that my brother could care less about his relationship with his mother, and I butted in and said that it's a lot more complicated than that. We also spoke about the 'bus ticket' issue back in June. He said that had he known, he wouldn't have thought twice about buying me the ticket. To me, John seemed like a simple guy with genuine intentions, and I told him I was glad that he was there to take care of my mother. We ended our conversation on a good note.

"John just texted me and said that Mom wants to know what her two sons think about her being in the hospital," my sister said. I took it as a shock and, it made me skeptical.

"I thought she couldn't speak," I said.

The next morning, I got a text saying that my mother had recovered fully and was exiting the ER. "They don't know what happened, but they're glad it's over. It sure was scary."

THEN CHRISTMAS CAME

One of the great mottos in the Coleman house was "no bullshit". And I wasn't going to let anything come in and ruin my Thanksgiving with them. I was surrounded by joy and honesty, and not even my mother could make me feel shame. The food, the people, the wine, the laughter and hugs; this is what Thanksgiving is all about.

Back in a routine, my mail route eventually doubled, and soon I was driving 8 hours a day, double what I'd done before. Along with this came more pay, and the ability to save up for my next adventure. Now I had even more time to think about things, as well as to plan the trip.

Around this time, I had an epiphany, and it was one of the greatest feelings I've had in life. Simple though it was, it felt tremendous. And as tremendous as it was, it wasn't an answer as much as a clear understanding of a 'steppingstone'.

My epiphany was a sense of purpose, and the purpose I found was that the only important thing in my life was to practice compassion. It was really that simple. To practice compassion using the tools that I had been given: music, writing, conversation. And during that moment, I realized that every purpose has its place, and that would be the next steppingstone: to find a place for my purpose, wherever it might be. The feeling from this experience never wore off. It still feels great to this day, because once you've found something you can say you're willing to die for, life becomes much more fulfilling.

Christmas was getting closer, and the rest of the family would soon be staying at the house. I was a little nervous, because I was concerned that maybe Mike's children would be a little annoyed that some 'dude' had moved into their father's home. Shortly after they got there, I found that this wasn't the case at all – they made me feel just as welcomed as their parents had.

I have to say that celebrating at their place was the greatest Christmas I had ever had. There wasn't one dull moment, no fights, no drama, and as Mike liked to say, "no bullshit". I can't describe how great it made me feel. My life was truly changing.

On Christmas day I bought my plane ticket to Sweden. The family knew I was going on a trip eventually, and they knew not to burden me with gifts that I couldn't use. They did however buy me gifts of chocolate and greetings cards, and I couldn't believe it, and I was even given money in these cards. Again, the generosity.

I bought my ticket to Sweden, and then to Finland, Germany, and Spain. I was going to plan this trip as I saved money. It was going to be a one-way journey around the globe, to end up teaching English in South Korea.

I decided that once I got to Spain, I would cycle across Spain up to Brussels. My heart pounded as I bought the ticket, because that was it. I was definitely going. I guess you could say it was my Christmas present to myself. Not so much the ticket, but the decision to embark on the greatest journey of my life thus far.

FROM HONESTY AND COMPASSION

The day after Christmas, my mother called me and left a message saying that I needed to call her. I called her back, and an unpleasant conversation ensued. "Thanks for calling me to say Merry Christmas," she said.

"I'm sorry mother, I meant to call you, but I got caught up in a lot of things yesterday. I meant to call you, but I'm glad I'm talking to you now."

"How many phone numbers do you have? I never know what number to call."

"I have the same phone numbers that I've had for the past several months. The same two."

"Well, I have to go, I'll call you back later," she said.

I went to the gym. I had started to seriously train, to prepare for my cycling journey. I wanted to build up muscle mass in my upper body, because the last time I'd gone on a cycling trip, my biceps became the size of my wrists – and I have small wrists.

I was sitting on a weight bench doing curls when I got a phone call from my mother. I answered the phone and she immediately tried to start an argument. As her speech became more vulgar and rapid, I set the phone down and continued to do curls. I picked up the phone when I was done, and she finished yelling and I hung up. I texted her back saying, "I think we got disconnected. I'm sorry you're upset. I hope you feel better."

After returning from the gym, I showed Peri some of the texts my mother had sent me. She hugged me and said she was sorry. It felt good to be in her arms, because she, too, knew what it was like to suffer, even though she might not have experienced the same things that I had.

I told her and Mike, "Well at least there was 'no bullshit' during Christmas."

The first day of 2015 came along. I got out of a bed feeling energized and started my day. Later that day, I picked up my computer and started to write on my website, 'cultsurvivor.com'.

I wrote about ideas of honesty, acceptance, and compassion. For some reason I felt compelled to write. The next day I wrote again, and the day after that. And then I realized I had started writing on the first day of the year, like a subconscious new year's resolution (which I don't believe in anyway). Nonetheless, I said to myself, "Why not keep writing every day for this month?"

And so I did. I wrote from my heart, every morning from that day on.

Every day, seven days a week, I would wake up, write, go to the gym, work, come home, visit and/or read, and sleep. That was it.

I thought to myself that if I was ever going to reach anyone, my best chance of doing it would be through actions of compassion, and the only way I would discover compassion in its fullest form would be through practicing self-honesty and self-acceptance. "How can I be honest with others, or accept others, if I can't do the same for myself?"

From that moment I even thought maybe it would be

the only way I could reach my parents. It might be my only chance to tell my parents who I had become, and who I wanted to become.

In the mornings I would write, and during drives I would think about what I wanted to write next. Often, I would call friends of mine and talk with them about these topics. I called my friend Thad a lot. Talking to him helped make the drives go by faster.

One day, I spoke with my father and we talked about these same big topics: acceptance, honesty, and compassion. We engaged in a very heartfelt conversation that brought me to tears in the end.

We expressed our love for each other, as well as our acceptance of each other in consideration of any actions that had taken place in the past. I felt, for the first time, that I was on the same page with my father.

And after that phone conversation, I said to myself, "Had I never had that conversation with my father, it would be a very sad thing."

BEGINNING THE NEXT JOURNEY

For years I had thought to myself while cooking meals, playing music, or engaging in deep conversations: "I wish my parents could see who I am."

I'd often wish that my mother or my father could see the person that I had become. The tastes I had developed, the dialogues I had engaged in, the music I had accomplished. I often thought about how great it would be to show my parents what I had blossomed into. And that there was no resentment, especially now, even though I was separated from them. I told my mother shortly after I'd started that I was writing, and that I'd be happy if she read it.

I continued with my routine and bought more tickets to further my travels. The month after I arrived to Spain, I'd be travelling from Italy to Egypt, then to Kenya, then to Nepal. However, after about two months of doing stream-of-conscious writing, I had a conversation with Mike, and as a wise elder, he helped put some things in my life into perspective.

The next morning, I decided that I would start to write this book, that now I was ready. Now I could dedicate time every day to writing about my life, growing up in a cult. But now it would be from a perspective of compassion. A perspective with the purpose of turning poison into medicine.

From there on out, I knew what my travels would be about. They'd be a time for me to potentially purge anything that might need to be purged, and to write this book. The story of a rather bizarre life filled with ups and downs. A life accompanied by handfuls of lemons, and some with jewels stuffed inside. A path in life that led to many doors, but where one door seemed the only right option – the door that opened to compassion. In a way, my journey began before I even left. My dreams became more bizarre, and more vivid, often filled with great symbolism. I had no idea what they were about, but I would surely remember them.

The middle of March came around, and I planned to visit my family in Michigan. It might be a long time before I saw them again. I also needed one extra document, should something happen to me during my long journey around the globe. I also knew that visiting the U.P. again would bring more drama between my mother and me to the surface, but I tried not to think about that.

I got back to the U.P. and I learned that my father was having health issues. He told me he had jaundice, difficulty breathing, constipation, and abdominal pain. He told me this over the phone while I sat in my aunt's living room.

"What have you been eating?" I asked.

"Oh you know, the meals that they serve at the House of Yahweh."

"What meals?"

"Well the meals that they prepare on the campgrounds," he said.

"What are you eating, Dad?" I asked firmly.

"Chicken, potatoes, and greens."

"What kind of work are you doing?"

"Oh, you know, the work that the House of Yahweh needs done."

"What work is that?"

"The work the needs to be done."

"Are you working with metals?" I asked, as I started to allow frustration into my voice.

"Yeah," he said.

"Which ones?" I asked, trying to determine whether this could be the cause of his jaundice.

"All kinds."

"Why can't you just be honest with me Dad?" I asked.

"You have your things going on, you're going to travel, why can't you just let me do my things?"

"Dad, I've been honest with you about everything in my life, more so than most people will likely ever be with anyone. Why can't you just be honest with me?"

"Well, you're better at it than I am," he replied. After hearing this, my heart began to sink.

"Well you can be too, Dad."

I didn't know what to think, but I was worried about my father. I told him he needed to go to the doctor, that he needed to get it checked out. I made him promise me that he would, and I said to him, "I don't want to go off on my trip, and learn later that you've ended up in a box. That won't happen, right?"

"No, it won't," he said.

THE GRASSHOPPER

I'd taken care of the last few things I needed to do in Marquette. I put some things into storage and gave away some to friends in need. I headed back to New York with some home-made tea from my friend Peter, and two meals of Rice Paddy directly from the owner, Aoy (arguably the best food in Marquette). I got back to New York and was in the process of preparing for my journey. My family and my friends were all happy for me and gave me great encouragement for what I was about to embark on. They knew as well as I did that this trip wasn't about having fun. It was definitely a learning experience, and we all knew it would be treated as such.

I eventually spoke with my mother while I was on the road. She insisted that I hadn't visited her this time because she wasn't one of my priorities. I figured she was trying to make me feel guilty.

I told her that I was still writing and she responded with, "Oh, I know all about what you're writing. You're writing about how bad your life was and 'poor and pitiful' you."

I said, "Well, no, that's not what I'm writing about."

"Oh I'm sure it's not."

"I don't believe that you've read it then, Mom."

"Well how do you know, Brandon?"

"Because I can observe my web traffic coming from Milwaukee," I said. That was followed by a sharp sudden sigh from my mother.

"Well I lied to you," she said. Then the conversation exploded into harsh words that I avoided listening to.

"I love you, I love you!" I shouted over the phone to my mother, repeatedly. I had no idea what else to say to her. I felt there was no use saying mean things, or calling her out on her actions in the past. There was simply no use. She told me crying that if I were to go on this trip, I would never see her again. She said she knew it for a fact. I told her that I didn't know how she could know such a thing, but I was sorry that she thought it.

I proceeded to go on with my day, and I continued the best that I could. As usual, I was happy to walk through that familiar main door again, where any weight that might be on one's shoulders gets lightened, if not completely removed.

Later that night I had a very vivid dream that involved my father. In the beginning of the dream, I was in Ed's house, and many members from the House of Yahweh were there. A dark feeling surrounded me, and I was compelled to warn everyone about the House of Yahweh. "I'm afraid things are getting really bad, and I'm afraid for you," I said to Evan in my dream, a young man who remained in the cult.

In the dream, he didn't seem to acknowledge that his brother had died in a car accident, but he had actually died nearly 20 years ago.

"You need to be careful," I warned the people in my dream.

Later in that dream I was sitting at a picnic table with

my father. I looked up at the pink and blue horizon over the trees, and I could see the house that I was just in. It was a blend of different houses where I had religious gatherings during my childhood. It was floating in the sky above the trees. The side of the house that was facing me was open, and you could see the floors with the people inside, like in a doll house.

Between my father and myself at the picnic table was a large paper bag filled with freshly cut vegetables. The bag was to my left, and we tipped it over to my right, and yellow peppers, red peppers, broccoli, celery, and rosemary rolled out to the center of the table. The rosemary was very vivid and stood out to me. I looked down again and saw a green grasshopper walking across the vegetables.

My father and I looked at each other and laughed. The sun shone down on us, and it was a very warm feeling. There was a lady walking away, maybe the one who had brought us the vegetables. Shortly after she left, a dog with antlers growing out of its head and back passed by us, and I was overwhelmed with a feeling of discomfort. The dog changed into a wolf, and I stood on the bench of the picnic table to tried and scare it away. It walked off, then onto a bridge in the distance, where it began to howl.

I looked at my father with worry and said, "He's going to call more wolves."

My father smiled and gently raised his eyebrows, and said calmly, "It's okay."

A GRAND JOURNEY

My last night in New York arrived; the next morning I'd be flying out. Earlier in the day, Mike saw me scrambling and said, "You need to relax. Everything will get taken care of." And I began to relax, and not to worry so much.

The excitement of what I was about to embark on, had me on edge. Not all my things were packed, so I felt the need to scramble. Also, I needed to cancel my car insurance, and plates, and all that other legal stuff before I left. Later that night, we had a Delmonico steak dinner with Mike's delicious home-made wine.

I sat with Peri and Mike individually that night, and I told them that if it weren't for them, I wouldn't be writing, and chances were that I wouldn't be on the spiritual path I was taking. Peri sat across the living room from me when I told her this, and she said she had no idea that they had such an impact on me. I told her that I wanted them to know that.

A little bit later in the evening I sat next to Mike. I looked over at him and told him that there wasn't a man I knew for whom I had more respect in this world. I shook his hand and a tear rolled down my cheek. Not only was Mike a hard worker, an artist and woodworker, a musician, a philanthropist, but he was an amazing parent. What he and his wife had accomplished collectively with their children was truly amazing. Two educated, cultured, hardworking and compassionate people came together and raised caring and undoubtedly brilliant children.

To me, that's amazing. It's like the golden apex of their collective and individual accomplishments. What could be more important in life to any who have children?

I went to bed late that night and woke up foggy. I slowly finished packing my 25-kg hiking pack, and then I was on my way to the train station. I packed one book, which is a lot for someone who isn't much of a reader – a friend had given me a copy of 'Walden' by Thoreau.

"To Brandon, at the beginning of a grand journey," my friend wrote.

My good friend Mark gave me a ride, and said he wasn't too fond of goodbyes, but would rather say "until next time". After a hug I was on my way to New York City to catch my flight.

Two nights before I left, I had been asked to give a short speech to a group of honorable men, in a large conference hall. They wanted to know about the journey I was about to embark on. I stood up and said I would be travelling around the world, writing a book about my life as well as my experiences on the journey. The purpose of the project was to serve as a beacon for any who it might help. That purpose became even more clear as my journey went on.

I arrived in Sweden and was greeted by dear friends with big smiles and warm hugs. To my surprise, I wasn't jet-lagged, and I was ready to explore and to enjoy my time with them. Later that night we prepared dinner, and there on the kitchen counter was a large sprig of fresh rosemary.

I learned that rosemary is very common in Sweden, but

that moment took me back to the dream I had before I left. That rosemary provided me with a feeling of comfort and of assurance that I was right where I was supposed to be.

WHAT ARE SIGNS?

Aside from the subject of my dream, and the feeling I had when I saw that rosemary while visiting Sweden, this wouldn't be the memoir I want it to be were I not to include a similar story that's stuck with me over time, even as I pursued my independent journey after leaving the cult.

I think the story works best if I begin with a conversation that I once had with a friend, a young man by the name of L.C. We were good friends in the cult.

L.C. was tall, thin, and kind, but he had a 'vibe' about him. He didn't look especially strong, but he was cut like a fighter and strong like a bear. He didn't like to fight, but he wouldn't hold back for a second if he had to.

He came to the House of Yahweh with some friends when he was about 19, and a couple of years later, there was a time when he left the compound for nearly a year. When he came back, he had this story to tell me: "Brandon, it was like I was constantly having nightmares of seeing the number 613, and knowing that I was moving away from the laws. I knew I needed to come back, and I couldn't handle the dreams any more. It was like Yahweh was telling me that I needed to go back."

It was a short conversation, but I never forgot it. This was well before I left. The number 613 in the House of Yahweh represent the 613 laws of Yahweh that had to be kept in order to enter the Kingdom of Heaven. Within that number, 6 is the number of man, and 13 is the number of God. I suppose you could ask a conspiracy theorist or a fortune teller, and they might tell you a lot more about that number. All I really know is what it meant to those in the cult.

Now, shortly after I left the cult, I started noticing the number in different places. Of course, whenever I saw it on a clock, I noticed it. But then odder things started to happen. I landed my first over-the-table job on that date. The next car I bought had that number on its odometer. I was at a party in college, and I looked at the clock on the oven around midnight, and the clock was broken but stuck on that time. No one knew my story of this number, because I kept it to myself. I didn't know whether it really meant anything, but it didn't bother me.

A few years later, I was speaking with an older gentleman who was affluent, and maybe a little superstitious or religious in some ways. I told him of my 'experiences' with this number and he said, "I know what that means." He never told me, but he told me eventually I would figure it out.

Then my ticket from Colorado to Ecuador was $613. Another time, I was walking through an underpass in Sudbury, Ontario, and saw the numbers spray-painted on a cement wall. And then there were odd times where I might take a wrong turn, or decide to go a different route, and I'd see the number on a license plate. It's unusual, I still feel, because the places that the number shows itself always strike me as a little uncanny.

As I said, I never was bothered by the number, but eventually I started to feel a kind of comfort in it. To this day, I don't know what it means, but whenever I see it in odd places, I hear a voice in my head saying that I'm where I'm supposed to be.

WHILE WRITING THIS BOOK

I was getting ready to leave Sweden, it was my last night there. I wouldn't be honest if I were to pretend that since I started writing about honesty, acceptance, and compassion, my life has all of sudden become free of emotional turmoil. Like all of us, I have my inner battles, and I knew that they wouldn't leave me on this trip. I knew that I would need to figure out how to let go of things.

The subjects that I wrote about, and the way I wrote about them, were in fact a way for me to try to overcome those inner battles. And although I can't say that the process of writing ended them, it surely has helped.

You see, I've struggled with loneliness, and confusion over relationships and how to go about them. But who doesn't feel the same struggle, at some point? I've felt intense emotions of jealousy that overtook me in the night and woke me with a pounding heart that wouldn't let me return to asleep. And because of what I see as the irrationality of these emotions, I've struggled to understand them. Indeed, I've done what I can to accept them.

I even confessed them to Mike one day, choking on my words as I expressed them. I feel that when you don't know what to do in such moments, the best thing you can do is to be as honest and compassionate as possible. At least, when I've been in such moments, I felt that to be my only chance.

So, this was also a part of my journey – to travel and find new perspectives with which to view myself. When a creator or artist of any type is in the midst of creating, they step back and observe their work from many different angles. This may be why it feels so frustrating when others spew out answers to our problems, because their perspectives are far from our own.

I continued to write throughout the journey. I wrote about the darkest moments of my life, and prepared myself to keep on writing about them. And here I am now, at the end, surprised to see that I'm writing about writing this book.

When I was in a train station in Stockholm, I wrote about the time my mother took me away from my father, and I found some sort of relief in that moment, and as I saw and felt that relief, tears poured down my face. Still, I didn't pause in my writing. I wrote through it, like I always do. A group of Swedish girls looked at me, and I knew they thought it was odd, but I didn't care. Just as when I play music, I know that there's no better place to play than in my heart. The same goes for writing. And shortly after I posted that particular portion of my writing on my blog, I got a message from a woman who I went to school with, who knew me then. She told me she was brought to tears when she read what I wrote.

I'm only human, but so are we all, and through honest expression we can, perhaps, all come together and discover that connection. This, too, is a purpose of this book.

8. A NIGHTMARE CAME TRUE

I was off to Finland and excited to discover something new about my roots. I thought it was special how the people there looked the same as they did from my hometown, how they sort of spoke the same, acted the same, had the same last names. The area even looked the same, and to my pleasant surprise, the food was better. But that was a given.

I met my family, and although distant in blood the spirit was very close to mine. Some of them treated me like a son, and some of them treated me like a brother. But in both regards, they made me feel I was being treated like a King, as I was often presented with an array of cheeses, wines, meats, vegetables, and other delicious foods. And although the foods were excellent, the most captivating moments were when they told me they could see my roots in me.

My cousin Teemu and I were in the sauna. A sauna is a relaxing place in the States, but in Finland it's a spiritual place, where you're naked and the same as anyone else. And again, as Mike would say, it's a place for no bullshit. Because when that happens, you get more steam.

'Sisu' had been a topic of discussion for me and many other Finns. Whether friends or family, all would say it's something difficult to describe. But then in the sauna, I had a discussion with Teemu and told him what it had been like to tell my father that I was never going back to Texas. That I would rather burn in hell than to continue with something that I didn't believe in. In that moment I knew that I was giving up my father, and forcing him to give me up, if he chose to stick with his beliefs.

"That's Sisu," said Teemu, and that's when the meaning of that word finally made perfect sense to me. Because what I felt during that experience – a feeling that you know in life, but you can't describe. In Brazil, they say "saudate".

Along with learning about my roots, another topic of discussion was suicide. Finns have a very high rate of suicide, most likely related to a brutal history paired with brutal conditions, and a sudden shift into modern times, where the individual need not live such an extreme life just to survive. In those extreme conditions, there's neither a time nor purpose to self-reflect or to reveal emotions. Maybe that's why after living with Mike and Peri, all those emotional struggles that I hadn't had the time or capacity to deal with finally surfaced, because my host family provided the emotional and physical space for that.

The topic of suicide was a dark one, because I've battled with those feelings myself in the past. Although dark, it was a necessary discussion for me to have with people in Finland.

The day that I left Finland, I received a message on my phone. It was my father, and he told me that he'd got his MRI results back, and that everything was fine. He said that all of his problems were likely caused from stress, and that he just needed to relax and take it easy.

"Where are you in the world?" he asked with a hint of laughter in his voice.

This journey had been filled with vivid dreams packed

with much symbolism. I had a very vivid one in Estonia. I was next to Mike, and he had his right hand wrapped around the back of my neck. It was like he was hugging me, and caring for me. It was odd, but an incredibly comforting feeling.

After a long night in Munich I got to Spain and found a hostel to sleep at. The next day I organized the time to pick up my bike, the following day. So on my third day in Spain, I built my bike right inside of Customs, and I was getting excited to start my long cycling trip across Europe.

I walked around Madrid that night, visited with friends, had drinks and went to bed around midnight. Within a few hours of being asleep I felt something touch my foot, and I jumped almost completely out of bed. Looking around with my hands flat on the bed sheets, I couldn't see anything or anyone. I went back to sleep, woke up around 7:00 a.m., picked up my phone and found several messages. One was from my aunt. She said I needed to call her.

"Fuck," I said as I got out of bed. I knew it was about my father. I knew he was gone.

I walked down to the lobby of the hostel and called my aunt. "It's about your dad, they found him hanging from a rope in a shed."

She broke into tears over the phone. I cried as well. Tears poured relentlessly down my face, since I couldn't have imagined that this would be the scenario of how my father would die. We talked and cried and talked and cried. Filled with misery, disbelief, and blame for the House of Yahweh, our worst fears had come true. That he would move down to Texas, and that we would never see him again.

At the same time, my worst fear concerning my trip and this book also came true. That I would have to write about my father's death before I finished the book.

I called my friends, my family. Those who could answer were roused from sleep. "I wish I could be there to hold you," said Mike, somehow reminding me of that dream. I walked up and down the streets of Madrid with tears pouring down my face. I didn't even know where I was going to stay that night, but I didn't care. The hostel was booked, but I would sleep in the street. I just didn't care.

I didn't know if I would even go back for the funeral. I was angry. I was torn. In shock. I kept walking, kept smoking cigarettes, and I tried to embrace as much about this situation as I could. I needed to feel it, and I needed to let it out. It was as if all my writing about honesty, acceptance, and compassion was done in preparation for this moment.

"This can only happen once," Mike reminded me.

I visited the Prado, knowing that it was the reason I'd come to Madrid in the first place. Although I say I wasn't sure whether I was going to go back to bury him, deep down I knew that I would. I just didn't know how it was going to work.

Was the House of Yahweh going to take control over everything? Had they already seized his belongings, like they'd done with so many other people?

Wait a second – why the hell would someone always so

worried about health, so they could live a long life, all of a sudden kill himself, out of the blue? Too many questions, many of which will never be answered.

I was supposed to meet with a couch-surfer that day, and speaking with her helped. I told her I was having a really bad day, and she was thinking that I simply couldn't find a place to stay. When I expressed my news she hugged me, and it felt so good to have a hug at that moment.

I finished my non-alcoholic beer and walked around with her for a bit. Later that night, I found a piano, and playing also helped. I went back to the hostel, grabbed my things, and made it to another place where I'd be sleeping.

The next day I went for a run, and then I sat down and wrote about my experience, and everything that I had learned. I wrote it under a post called "A Message of Love."

A MESSAGE OF LOVE

It sounds arrogant to say this, but I've found my purpose in life. As big and grand as it may sound to some, what it really means to me is something very simple. My purpose is something that I'm willing to die for.

Honestly. It's something that I am able to fall back on, during any time of need. Even during the darkest of times, I'm able to create a fire from this purpose to push myself further in the direction that I'm headed.

Not too long ago, thousands of people lost their lives in an earthquake in Nepal. So many people are hurting, and I feel for them. Tremendously. I feel that when dark times come over me, there's always a chance that I will lose sight of what's important, and I guess in my current situation, I'm thankful that all my other superfluous issues have been rendered silent. I'm pushing further in the direction of pursuing my purpose: to practice compassion to its fullest extent.

Nothing, and I mean nothing is more important in this life than having a positive influence on one's surroundings. Selflessness is the purpose of existence, and the key to discovering the strongest power of existence.

I think I could say I suffered a great loss a few days ago. But the truth is, I didn't lose anything. A couple months ago, I had a conversation with my father, and it went something like this:

"Dad, I want you to know that if it wasn't for you, I wouldn't be pursuing a life of honesty, and a life filled with compassion.

Because of you, I have a deep love for all those around me, and I know that you did everything you could for me. You taught me a lot, and even though you weren't perfect, and even though you made some mistakes, I love you, and I'm very happy that you were my father."

And then he told me:

"When I was a young boy my father was very violent, and there were times that we didn't know if he would kill us. He had a big alcohol problem, and he would beat your grandmother. I was scared, and I hated it. I could never want this for anyone, and so this is why I believe in kindness. I'm sorry I couldn't have done more for you, and I'm sorry that I beat you that one time when you were a boy. It hurt me bad, but I love you."

My father was moving to Texas to be with the cult, and his whole family was worried that this might be the last time we would see him. After he moved, he became stressed out and started having what seemed to be severe health issues. He thought that he just needed to do some cleanses to fix his problems, and he really didn't want to go to the doctor. His whole family tried to encourage him to go to the doctor. He had jaundice and difficulty breathing, for crying out loud! So eventually he went. He went to get an MRI, and according to his friends, he seemed cheerful about the results.

About two days later, this is what happened:

He was working on an air compressor with one of his friends in the House of Yahweh. This was happening in a shed where he'd been working on the roof a day or two before. His friend Dan left the shed to work on another project, and he was gone for about an hour. When Dan returned to the shed, the doors were locked and the lights were off. He broke open the door and found a 6-foot blue ladder lying on the floor and my father's body hanging above it.

I've thought about this for going on three days now. Death is complicated. Suicide is even more complicated, and suicide that takes place inside an extreme fundamentalist cult maximizes the complications.

Dan called one of the elders, then the elder called Yisrayl Hawkins for instructions. The priest told Dan to go look at the body and to check his pulse, to see if he was alive. Dan said the body felt cold and that there was no pulse. Whatever happened directly after or before that is unknown. Then the priest, David Heimerman, called the owner of the property where it happened and instructed him to call the police. These are among the complications that a cult can impose on death.

Several fire trucks, a local judge, squad cars and EMTs were all on the scene within minutes. Pictures were taken, keys were taken, and everything seemed to be on lockdown. It was a shock to everyone.

I can't imagine what my father was going through. Of course I wish he would've called me one last time. Of course I wish I could have seen him one last time. But the truth is, I know he loved me, and that's why I don't feel like I've lost.

Suicide can make anyone think that the doer was a coward, but how can anyone possibly know the deep inner struggles of another? My father suffered from unknown things. My family and I understand that. However, now we can know that he's no longer suffering.

It's been a few days now, and my eyes still hurt. There are still tears that are working their way out while I write this. People tell me that they can't imagine what I'm going through, and I can't imagine how long this pain is going to last, because there are so many good memories of this good man. He was a loving man, who loved to laugh, who loved to work, and most importantly, who loved to love. He truly is the reason my intention in life is to turn poison into medicine.

If I could give one message to my father right now, it would be that I love you, and I forgive you.

RETURNING TO THE CULT GROUNDS

Within a day, I had made the decision that I would go back to bury my father. My mother had called me a few times, saying that I needed to call her. I was a little taken back that my mother wanted me to talk to her. I was caught up with so many things, and it was hard to focus on one, especially something that someone "needed" from me at that moment. Eventually I spoke with her and she said that if there were anything she could do to help, I shouldn't hesitate to ask.

I decided to ask her to help me with getting my ticket to Chicago, from Madrid.

I found a ticket for under $500, and to my surprise, my mother offered to pay for the ticket, so I could come back to the States to bury my father. That was the biggest financial help I had ever gotten from my mother.

The plan was that I would meet my mother, my aunt, and my sister before my aunt, sister and I drove down to Texas. My mother gave me the impression that she wanted me to spend a night or two with her, but I didn't have the time. I had a tight itinerary already, and this interruption would end up costing me two weeks. I told her I'd be able to meet her at the airport to have lunch with her.

As the time got closer, she told me that she wouldn't be able to drive down to Chicago because she wasn't feeling well, and that she would meet my aunt in Milwaukee to give her the money for my plane ticket. I told her I'd let her know what day I'd be back in Chicago before I left again, so we could see each other. She agreed and asked me to keep in touch while I was down there.

When my aunt and sister came to pick me up, we didn't waste any time. We headed straight down to Abilene, Texas. We left Chicago at 3:00 p.m. and arrived in Baird' County the next day around noon. We went right to the sheriff's office, where they had my father's police report, wallet, and keys to his property.

We were all tired, sweaty, and sad, and tears often accompanied sweat as we went through this journey. The sheriff handed me the packet of papers and my stomach felt like a heavy weight, hanging from a rope attached to my throat. I read the first page of his preliminary autopsy report, and I saw the pictures of his property, located near the House of Yahweh grounds. There was a big "Peaceful Solution" sign on his property, a subject he seemed to fully stand by.

And then there were three pictures of his dead body hanging from a black and orange rope. The first picture was from a distance, the second was from the same angle but closer, with his head turned away. Then the last picture was a close-up of his face. Even though my father was clothed, there was a sense of nakedness about him, with his pants wet with urine. My aunt grabbed me and held me. We all looked at the pictures and cried.

We asked why, we had words of denial and words of love. This was the beginning to the end of finding our closure to this dark occurrence.

From the sheriff's office, we went to the funeral home

to speak with the mortician, the justice of peace, and then to the scene of the incident. Dan was the person who had found my father, and he was the second person there when we arrived.

I asked him how he was, and he said, "Well, I didn't cry the first day, I cried the second day, but I haven't cried since."

Before I spoke with Dan I spoke with Don, a man in his early 70s and the owner of the property when it had happened. I remembered him from the Wisconsin branch of the House of Yahweh, from when I was a child. I asked what happened, and the two men, Don and Dan, both said it just happened out of the blue. My father and Dan had been working on an air compressor, and that Dan stepped away from the scene for a couple hours, then came back and found my father hanging. Dan said that my father had been encouraged to empty out his bank account before getting the MRI done; that way, they couldn't take his money directly out of the bank, should he need a big operation. This was their reasoning on why my father was told to do this. They then told me that he had a strong-box on his property with all of his money in it.

We packed up some things in my father's vehicle and drove it off of Don's property, and headed to my father's place. We wondered if we would find anything there. We heard rumors from people who had left that Yisrayl Hawkins and the elders were known to go through the belongings of a deceased member and take anything of value. I even heard Mattithyah Arcemont say this years ago:

"It all belongs to Yisrayl anyways. Those heathens will never get what belongs to him."

Even the judge said that Hawkins was notorious for this, but that such behavior died down after he was convicted on charges of polygamy. He didn't want more bad publicity.

Along with not knowing whether my father's valuables would be missing, we didn't know if anything might happen to us, once the sheriff left us. The entire time, in the middle of those backwoods of Texas, we felt watched. And people continually driving past in their rusty pick-up trucks more or less confirmed this.

Looking through his belongings, we didn't find anything of value. We decided that we would have to come back later and spend a couple of days going through everything. One thing is for certain, there was no strong-box, and no sign of any suicide note or medical records. All these things were missing.

"Maybe he had some of his things on the bus that he stayed in during the feasts," I said to myself.

I asked the sheriff to call the elder Matt Stubbs to see if he would give us permission to go onto the compound where the bus was. Matt said that he'd call back later, and within a couple of hours he told the sheriff that we could go in, under his supervision.

After we left my father's property, we headed back to the funeral home. There we saw Dale's body, and later we were picked up by Matt Stubbs.

Seeing my father would be the second-to-last thing I'd

have to do, and I knew it wouldn't be easy. Bearing the pain, I more or less floated through these actions and took everything in as well as I could. It didn't look like him, and it barely felt like him when I touched his face. Again, we all cried and held each other. It would have been incredibly hard for any two of us to have dealt with this. We all needed each other there.

9. TWISTING THE KNIFE

Matt (a cult leader and possibly the next sheriff of the county) pulled up in a somewhat new silver Suburban. He got out of the vehicle with a slight smirk on his face. I had no idea what was going to happen, or what he was going to say, but the truth is, I didn't care one bit. I wasn't about to start a confrontation, but as the trip with Matt went on, I sensed that he wanted just that.

My family and I got into the Suburban and headed to the compound. It had been 11 years since I'd last been on those grounds. I never planned on going back, and I surely never wanted to. Here I was reminded of the recurring dreams I'd had since I left. Being on the compound, and wishing I wasn't there.

"Do you have any idea why your father would've done this?" Matt asked as he turned to me with that slight grin on his face.

"No idea," I said.

Matt didn't seem to show any signs of empathy at all, and I felt that I really needed to bite my tongue most of the time I was with him. We arrived at the grounds, got to the bus, and went and looked around, while Matt waited outside for us. Again, we didn't find anything.

We looked through my father's belongings but found nothing concerning his medical condition, and certainly no strong-box. I looked in what used to be his liquor cabinet, and sure enough, it still was that. My father hadn't drunk for years, so it was a surprise to find his liquor cabinet fully stocked. I grabbed a bottle of rye whiskey and took a large gulp to calm my nerves, since I was becoming angry and impatient with the whole situation.

I told Matt that my father had another trailer, and that I'd like to take a look in it before I left the grounds. I pointed out where it was – "Just right over there, not even 100 yards."

"Let's drive over there," he said.

"Okay," and we drove a few feet. I felt as if he wanted to give the appearance that there was something he was hiding.

Soon Mattithyah Arcemont showed up. We had been friends in the past, but of course I was a heathen. "Long time no see Brandon." As I approached him and gave him a big hug. I'm not sure what I was thinking.

"Indeed," I responded.

"Too bad it had to be under these circumstances," he said, looking down and smiling slightly.

"Yeah, it's too bad. It's a sad story," I said.

Both of the Matts stood next to each other as they watched us go through things in the trailer.

"So you're an elder now, eh, Mattithyah?" I asked as he leaned up against a semi.

"We're called Kahans now. You're a bit behind on the times. You know Brandon, I read almost your entire blog. You're really behind on the times," he said confidently.

I guess he didn't know that it's possible to watch web traffic on a blog, and see how much time people are spending on the site from places like Clyde. So what he said seemed to me silly more than anything.

"That's good, I'm glad you're reading it," I said.

"You knew he was a Kahan," said Stubbs.

"No, I didn't, I just assumed that he would be by now. I guess you more or less confirmed it."

As we were getting ready to leave, Matt Arcemont told me to check out the Peaceful Solution website, and I told him that I had. "I'll make you guys some links to that website." I said to him as he got in his car.

"Oh, you don't need to do that, I'm sure there's already a lot," he said as he left.

The three of us rode back to the funeral home with Matt Stubbs.

"So what are you doing these days?" Stubbs asked.

"I'm a jazz musician and a writer," I said.

"Is that what you're doing in Madrid?"

"I've been travelling, writing a book, and playing music wherever I go," I said.

Stubbs went on about remembering how I played music when I was younger, and he reminded me of another saxophone player who used to be in the House of Yahweh. And then we started talking about the book that I was writing.

On a side note, the writing of this book was a big concern for those who were close to me.

"Could someone come after you for this, Brandon?"

"You need to be careful, Brandon, you're in a journalist's position right now."

Those thoughts were already in my head. Especially when I went down to Texas.

"Can I trust Stubbs?" I asked an ex-member via text.

I received a reply to that text, just as I was getting in the door of his vehicle. "No! Absolutely not. He ran me off the road the other night!"

It's hard to predict what could occur in such a situation. Odds are, nothing will happen. But in the backwoods of Texas, people talk with an accent that at times requires subtitles. A murder case getting solved is probably a rare occurrence. I'd heard rumors of other ex-members receiving death threats.

But thanks to the numbness caused from seeing my father, just minutes before, I was more concerned with the abundance of possibilities than any physical damage. In the moment, you might say I didn't really care.

I thought deeply about the fear that this group used to control its followers. A big part of using fear to get people to believe you is convincing them that they need to fear the consequences of disobedience, more than anything else. Playing at extremes is how I see it.

Fear can set up a psychological playground in the mind, where people need to continually run away from a made-up sense of evil. If they resist temptation, they'll receive unimaginable rewards. And within that playground, excitement is what draws the individual away from their own logic. The tricky part is that people often have their own demons, and sometimes these demons are really intense. Maybe a man who was a heroin addict most of his life, and who lost his son in a car accident, speaks with a priest while in prison. And during that conversation, this man finds Nirvana. Although it's completely made up, and sold on material values, this man becomes a soldier for this priest and religion. He'll now dedicate his work to his faith, and give as much money as they encourage him to do.

The ability or inability of an individual to reason under difficult circumstances can sometimes be a determining factor in whether or not they will join a cult. Some of us have been in difficult moments where we feel that we need an answer quickly. It can be difficult to step away from that feeling and say, "Wait a second, I'm just going to live in this moment, and simply 'feel' what life is handing me right now, even though it hurts tremendously."

I think it's safe to argue that trying to manipulate a person under such circumstances is nothing other than true evil. It is an act that removes someone completely from their social setting, outside of their will. They're stolen from their family and they're stolen from themselves.

For me, the ability to see (deconstruct this evil) in my mind – how, when, or why people get caught up in these walks of life – is the medicine derived from the poison that the House of Yahweh gave me. Many have said that Yisrayl Hawkins stole their children, their wife, their brother or sister. Many people have said that Yisrayl Hawkins stole their money, their house, or their dead relative's belongings. Many have said these things quietly, amongst themselves, but never in the public eye. And let me tell you another thing about the fear that's learned in the House of Yahweh:

it's planted deep, and the worst thing we were taught about 'fall-aways' is that they spoke against Yisrayl Hawkins. That was a big insurance policy imposed against the House of Yahweh members.

"You know, Stubbs, when I left, I left quietly, and I didn't try to take anyone with me."

He had his right arm extended over to the steering wheel. He looked over his right shoulder and said quietly, "Well. It's a good thing you didn't."

I find that the most beneficial way to look at fear is this: I ask myself, "Do I fear?"

If yes, then, "What do I fear? Am I afraid I'll suffer?"

Then I think, "I'd better not fear that, because then I'm already suffering."

I said to Stubbs, "You know, I tried to believe in many things about the House of Yahweh, I paid my tithes, but I just didn't agree with it. Simply put, Yisrayl Hawkins said things that I just don't agree with. And I'd rather burn in the Lake of Fire, instead of following something I didn't believe in."

He didn't have much to say after that. He dropped us back off at the funeral home, and we left to find a hotel.

THROUGH THE MOTIONS

Perhaps the only nice thing about that hot, exhausting day was the air-conditioning in my aunt's van. The heat wore us down, we were tremendously tired from the drive, and our emotions were shaken as much as they ever had been. We did our best to stay joyful, and for the most part we did. But every now and then, our company was interrupted by a random outburst of tears. But this had been happening from the beginning, ever since we found out.

We found a hotel with a pool and managed to get a good night's rest. The next day we were off to sift through my father's belongings in hopes that we'd discover the few sentimental things that he had left. Although we'd slept and rested fairly well, we were still emotionally exhausted. None of us needed to be pushed in any way. I knew that however we went about doing this, we needed to do it as a team.

We had a lot of work to do. My father had two storage units, the 40-foot kind used for international shipping, filled with odds and ends. Tools, shelving, a table from his sister, a cabinet I built when I was 14. I was surprised to see that there. Pictures, books, more tools, House of Yahweh literature, more house of Yahweh literature, and even a picture of my father standing with Yisrayl Hawkins.

During this time I thought, "You know, I just don't fucking get it. He probably paid about a million dollars throughout his life to the House of Yahweh. He kept the laws they told him to keep, down to the finest detail. Probably better than most elders there do. He bought all the books, he retired from the mine, and here I am hoping to the heavens that I can find his sterling silver wedding ring, with nothing other than sentimental value."

The only way for me to get it was to understand how such a kind and diligent person like my father can be taken advantage of. It makes me dance between sadness and anger in my heart, and I'm not sure I'll ever get over it.

My father's two shipping containers were on an acre plot known as 'the 88'. A place where no one who's not from the House of Yahweh likes to go, or even would go. The ground is muddy when wet, and hard as a rock when it's dry. There's about a month of green, and the rest of the year, 5-foot tall bushes covering the landscape turn brown and grey. The land is desolate. There's nothing, and it's surrounded by surveillance cameras so House of Yahweh security knows what's going on at all times.

Yes, we all felt that we were being watched, like when seeing the same people drive by several times.

I had to do something to help me get through the day, and as we started to go through his things, I let myself feel anger instead of sadness. Anger at the House of Yahweh, anger with my father (selfish anger, that is), and anger at what might have happened to his belongings.

I began to go through his clothes in hopes that I would find something important, something that would provide an explanation.

"Can we not go through his clothes right now?" said my aunt with tears in her eyes. I began to calm down a bit.

We went through as many of his belongings as we

could. Almost everything. But to our dismay there was no strong-box, no letter, and nothing that might offer an explanation of why this happened.

10. QUESTIONS AND DECISIONS

After we spent hours and hours going through his belongings, we began to have a conversation about where we'd have him buried, and that was one of the hardest decisions we had to make. None of us wanted to be the one to make the decision, but it had to be made.

We wanted to respect his wishes, but we also wanted to keep other family members in mind. He wanted to be buried next to his wife, but that was on property owned by the cult.

"Do we bury him in another cemetery? Do we take him back to Michigan?" All these questions were on our mind, and we had no idea what to do. Expenses were also an issue, and taking him back to his hometown would not be cheap, so that was almost out of the question.

We eventually decided later that day that we'd have him buried next to his wife in the cemetery owned by Yisrayl Hawkins. This was far from an easy decision, but I guess you could say that my father didn't leave us in an easy position to make that decision. Again, he probably left a note if he actually did hang himself. And if he did, the House of Yahweh took that note.

It was most likely David Heimerman who would have taken a note, since he was the 'Kahan' on the scene, and he waited hours before he called Don Wordon and instructed him to call 911. That may be the reason David wouldn't speak to any of us. We called the funeral home and told them where we'd have him buried, and we scheduled for

10:00 a.m. the next day. By that time, I had already been preparing things to say over his body.

I knew this was going to be something of a 'redneck' funeral. It was inexpensive, in fact the cheapest it could be. We did have a granite tombstone made with his name on it.

At that cemetery they generally have nothing, or just the name Hawkins printed in cement. For me, all those things are superficial, and they really don't matter anyway. Even if he didn't have a tombstone, I would know where he is.

I made sure his body was centered in his grave and they lowered him into the ground. I also made sure it was me who picked him up in his casket, out of the coach. I wanted to be the one, and no one else. I also wanted to be the one to say the words. Perhaps I felt that I was the only one in the family who could muster a few of them, but I certainly didn't want anyone else talking about my father. I didn't want any religious jargon. This wasn't about religious faith; this was simply about a family's love for someone who they knew was a beautiful person.

In the House of Yahweh, they believe that when someone dies, they simply go to sleep, to be awakened at one point during the resurrection. This is why they don't have funerals or tombstones, and perhaps this is why none of the people who were close to my father showed any signs of an ability to grieve. I wrote about my father's burial in "A Message of Love, Part 2" a few days after it happened. He was buried on the 1st of May, 2015.

Preparing myself to perform the ceremony proved to be the most draining thing I'd ever done in my life.

Afterwards I was the most exhausted I had ever been. But I knew I needed to do it. I knew I needed this experience to be difficult and painful, if I were to deal with it appropriately. And because I have, I'm now able to sit calmly and write about it. With that, it certainly changed me. How could it not?

After his funeral, we continued with the logistical work of trying to get his electricity turned off, and also trying to learn about his MRI results. The secretary where he got the test done said it shouldn't be a problem, but this seemed odd to us. Despite our doubts, we were still desperate to learn of the results, and we were hoping that we'd get some information. To our expected dismay, we were left with no information, making the situation permanently frustrating. In any suicide, people will say that there's no closure. That's because we always feel like there's something we could have done, something we should have known about the other person. But in this situation, too many pieces to the puzzle were missing, and there's only one group of people who have the answers, but they're not talking.

"How on Earth do we get the authorities to investigate this further?" His family and friends continue to wonder.

AFTER THE BURIAL

We got back to the hotel after running around, trying to find answers.

We decided it was enough for the day. For me it definitely was. I needed to do something that would take my mind off things, and thankfully there was a friend in town who I was able to meet with. We met for the first time in Marquette, because I made a joke about the House of Yahweh. She laughed like she knew what I was talking about, and she did.

I made a joke to her this time saying, "See, the House of Yahweh brought two heathens together again. What do you know?" We both laughed over a few drinks that night. I think it's fair to say that it was a well-deserved escape.

We had decided that we were going to head back the next day. I spoke with my mother on the phone again and told her how the funeral went. She expressed a lot of sadness in her voice. I told her that I would let her know when we were getting to Chicago. I was eager to get out of Abilene, but I think my sister and aunt just wanted to make a good start on the trip. We made sure my father's belongings were all locked up, then went to meet up with a friend from childhood before we left. He invited me to see another mutual friend who I hadn't seen for 11 years, and I agreed.

During that time, another ex-member who I'd been in touch with offered to drive an hour to see me, even if only for an hour. It was nice to see everyone, but like everyone seemed to be saying, "It's too bad it's under these circumstances." But frankly, I can't imagine why anyone would simply visit Abilene, Texas. My friend showed up on the property, and we chatted a while before heading to a local brewery.

I leaned up against a tree during our conversation, and looked down, and a green grasshopper jumped on my leg. "I guess the hard part's over," I said to myself.

We all headed towards the pub to have one last chat. The conversation led to concerns about the dangers that the House of Yahweh poses for its followers. I became fully convinced at that time that the House of Yahweh had become an unstable place.

We left, on our way to Wichita Falls. We spent a night there, another night in Missouri, making our way north to Chicago. We stopped again a couple of hours south of Chicago, and a friend of mine was expecting my call. I let him know what was going on. "Why not just come all the way to Chicago?" he asked. "Are you too tired? If you want me to come, I'll come."

Shortly after, he drove two hours to come and visit me. Almost exactly two hours after our phone conversation, he was there. I hadn't seen him since I lived in Ecuador.

Earlier that day I had texted my mother and told her that I'd be in Chicago the next day. The next day I received a bundle of texts from her, and my only conclusion was that she was having a bipolar episode. There was a long text that talked about the selfishness on my part, and how she forgave me for having a family in New York, and then cruel words that parents simply don't say to their children. I showed the text to my aunt and within seconds she started crying. "I'm sorry, Brandon. You sure don't have it easy."

I tried to explain to my mother that I didn't know the exact time I'd be in Chicago, and she insisted it was my fault that I didn't see her. I was completely baffled by this situation, because she didn't want to come see me in Chicago when I arrived, and now it had happened twice. And the bafflement didn't stop, because the last text she sent me was a message stating that she was disowning her son.

I said to her, "I'm not sure why a parent would ever let go of their children."

And there have been no words between us since. I hesitate to write this, but this book is the memoir of a 29-year-old, and this is something significant that happened, which parallels other moments in my past. I do love my mother. She taught me charisma, and how to dance. She told me about women, and in a roundabout way she showed me how to teach myself independence.

I love my mother, but I don't know how to love her except from a distance.

Finding the strength to let this rain roll off wasn't difficult. All I had to do was remind myself what the ropes felt like in my hand – the rope that my father hung himself with, and the ropes that I used to put him in the ground.

Soon I was on a plane back to Europe. I would eventually get back to writing my book, and furthering my journey. It's what my father would've wanted.

AN INTERLUDE

People have often told me, "You know, it's a good thing you got out when you did."

Unfortunately, this is very true, and it's true of potentially dangerous situations for many people. Rumors of domestic violence, extreme polygamy, questions of how cruelly young girls might be treated. The stress that the cult followers endure, leading to heavy psychological issues. Maybe this is what these types of sects tend to become over the span of five decades.

"The joy is gone, Brandon. There's no more joy. You remember what it used to be like. There was fellowship, there was laughter, music. But then the wall went up and everything started to go downhill. People are working seven days a week now. There's no day of rest anymore.

"I think that's what happened, Brandon. Your father started to wake up. He probably saw everything for what it was, and just couldn't take it. You know how your father was, He was more diligent than anyone. Not one person here can say anything negative about your father.

   — An Ex-member.

In the beginning I wanted to believe that my father committed suicide. It was easier for me to get through the initial trauma in believing it. But, there's just too much information missing from this puzzle. Not only in his death, but nearly every death that has happened near the compound, and nobody seems to know why. All I know is that in my father's case, the House of Yahweh was the beneficiary of his biggest financial asset; his retirement money from nearly 40 years at Cleveland Cliffs Inc, and that the man at the scene of his death, encouraged him to establish that a few years prior.

The evolution of small sects seems to be limited to few outcomes. The sect can come to an end through dissipation, or by an act of extreme consequence. This is the balancing act between the love of illusion and being consumed by it. Jim Jones and his Kool-Aid, Waco and the military tanks – both are examples of cults that we don't hear much about until the extremity reaches its apex.

I don't think any expert can predict when this will happen with any sect. What my friend said was true about the House of Yahweh having once been a joyful and pleasant place. In the beginning, there was excitement. Sure it was a little odd in many ways, but at that time there was cohesion. This eventually faded and started to become more extreme shortly before I left.

What I myself saw has allowed me to realize how individuals can be gradually swayed, over time, into doing things that at the beginning they wouldn't consider doing. One time, when I was younger, about 8 or 9, I asked my father, "Dad, what if they started hurting people, and they said we have to hurt ourselves? Would you follow them?"

"No, I wouldn't," he said.

I've heard a lot of rumors about that place – what things have become, and how the changes made around the time I left have had significant results. Imagine the intensity, the likely evolution, of practices that I spoke of earlier. What can possibly have become of those things now? Without actual proof, there's no way of knowing.

They do a good job of hiding behind their biggest project: The Peaceful Solution.

This is a claim to world peace, through their workshops. If that were true, why have over two-thirds of the sect left? Of course, we were always taught that three out of every four would turn away, but that's just a sophisticated way of saying, "Only 25 percent of you will believe this story." The ones who did decide to leave were simply told they weren't called or chosen, so essentially, they didn't even count in that equation. This adds to the alienation of ex-members. Not only from the group, but amongst themselves. They feel alone, and that their situation rightly separates them from every other ex-member. I'm not saying that's how it always is, but rather how it can be for some. Because in part, that's how it was for me.

This alienation works to the advantage of the sect as well, because by means of fear, they've already controlled the actions of soon-to-be ex-followers. It's hard not to see this as a strategic insurance policy. If the ex-members were to organize, it might just be enough to result in a safe dissipation of the group. Of course this sort of discussion would be seen in the House of Yahweh as an outright attack. We were told that Yahweh most punishes those who speak against Yisrayl and his teachings.

He is believed to be "The one who rules as Yahweh." So they're his teachings now. There's a series of books with that in its title.

I'm not 100% sure that bureaucracy allows such social manipulation to take place, but thanks to certain particular words on paper, sects like that of Jim Jones or Dave Koresh can't be stopped, or even investigated in the first place.

It's so easy to say, "Yeah, but polygamy is illegal." But multiple marriages do happen, and they'll continue to take place until the government stops them. The Mormons used to practice this, but then all of a sudden God told them it wasn't okay anymore. So they quit.

But how did they and other sects get away with it in the first place, and how long did they practice it? Bureaucracy is where it tends to end for those who have lost tremendous amounts to extreme sects. But again, if people would organize amongst themselves, then many reasonable goals can and will be achieved.

Many people have reached out to me, throughout this experience, and they've told me that they think I'm brave, and that I seem happy, and that they're happy for me. A lot of thought has gone into this project, and I want to say that for the most part, my life isn't currently filled with constant happiness. That being said, it's also not filled with disappointment or despair, or anything consistently negative. In a way, you could say that I don't believe in happiness – in a way.

In a certain light, I feel that if I believed in happiness, then I would equally believe in its opposite. Although there are moments when I feel happy, and there are moments when I feel sad, I spend most of my energy trying to accept each moment for what it is, being content with whatever is happening. Every moment is a passing thing, anyway, and it's difficult enough to try to grasp it while it's there. I think that maybe, if I ever lose track of feeling content, then I might easily get lost in total happiness or sadness. And I don't want to do that.

I guess the message that I'm trying to convey is that my life hasn't reached a "happy ending". And I'm okay with that. But trust me – I'm glad whenever people are happy for me. I want them to be happy, because I know very well the feeling I get when I see other people's happiness. It's great, and I do believe that true happiness is only real when shared.

Life is a journey, and oftentimes it seems like a puzzle with no solution. My life to this moment has been filled with an abundance of lessons. Indeed, it took me a decade to be able to sit down and write about my life growing up in a cult. It also took me the better part of a decade to let go of the resentment I felt for my mother. But it was in that same decade that I started to learn how to turn poison into medicine. By no means do I claim to have done that with every ailment that life has handed me, but at least I can say that I'm conscious of it now; and so I often contemplate how to turn those ailments into cures.

Despite my past in a doomsday cult, and despite my complicated relationship with my mother, the opportunities that my journey through life have presented me have allowed me to experience a lot in 29 years.

As I struggled to find myself emotionally, and as I practiced my honesty out loud (so to speak), I ended up sharing a lot of myself with many people, and as a result, many people have shared a lot with me.

I have seen people at their weakest, most exposed moments. Recently I've looked back on the relationships I've had with people, moments I've shared with them and the things that they opened up to me. I'm very thankful for these experiences, because not everyone has the fortune to take part in so many different situations early in life. And even though many of those relationships no longer exist, the lessons that I learned about mutuality remain deep in my heart. Very few people have seen me at my weakest moments, but it's these experiences that make me want to continue down the path of compassion.

Happiness exists, and so does sadness, but either can be deceptive.

As they say in Brazil, "Do not curse the sun, and do not curse the rain." Or just as Icarus was instructed to not fly too high or too low, I feel the same with sadness and happiness. Yes, there are times when I've gotten stuck in the rain, without an umbrella. But now that I'm getting a little older, I can sometimes find more patience for standing back and watching the clouds before it rains; or before I get lost in the sun's warmth.

So I suppose I just want to make it clear to my friends and readers that I haven't reached a state of constant happiness. Instead, all I hope to achieve is this: to let everyone know that I'm still right here, I'm still Brandon from the U.P.

Like many others, I'm still working on things that I suppose many others are also still working on. I hope we can all somewhat feel connected by our similarities. Because I believe that's what happiness is all about: connection.

CONCLUSION

The whole purpose of writing this book was to function as a beacon for those who have been in any sort of similar situation. I remember my father showing me a picture of a lighthouse when I was a child. "You see that light coming out, that's you, a beacon light. That's what your name means." And when I think about it, the purpose of a lighthouse is simply to say "Hey, I'm here, you're there; this is where we are." The lighthouse, being an inanimate object, doesn't know what else is out there, it doesn't know what ships might pass, or who's on them. The lighthouse just sits there and does what it was built to do. When my father told me this, it stuck with me and grew with me. Like it was something that I felt I needed to live up to.

Over the past decade, more meaning came with this thought, and the act of helping others couldn't be more appropriate. I've always had a loudmouth, somewhat random at times, but honest none-the-less. Sometimes my words of honesty were clearly there to offer some form of beacon to open ears, but many times those words were, and still are a beacon for myself. So in that sense, this book is also a beacon for me as well; a way to take a large portion of my life, or my whole life rather, lay it out, and use as a recipe for the strongest medicine I've made thus far. Any effort to heal others will also heal ourselves. People have mentioned to me that they wonder what it takes to make someone turn over to the dark side. What makes someone stay a benevolent person when they have been chewed up by the wolves so many times. I'm not sure I will ever have an answer for that. All I know is that I desire a healthy future. One that's filled with selfless compassion and never-ending growth in wisdom.

However, there are sometimes situations in life where someone might do something that in the end, causes suffering. Like drinking too much, for example. It seems fun and enjoyable, but later leads to suffering. The key is always to look inside and to probe at what is really the source of suffering. And then, change it, if one so desires. In terms of me satisfying my material desires, be it from nice cars/clothes to sexual encounters, drugs and religion, those only may seem like easy solutions to problems. They really don't matter; none of them. But to satisfy that burning desire to have a presence in this world, to feel my direction, and to know that I'm applying my purpose; nothing could mean more to me in life.

What I'm about to say is very controversial, however I believe it to be true; Organized religion is a bad thing. For all people, for all nations, and even though there are moments when people are brought together over it, or the times that mends holes in social fabric, in the end, organized religion is something that human kind needs to move past. It's not only the deaths caused by religion, but the encouragement of separation between nations. Religion produces prejudice, racism, breeds closed-mindedness, and at the same time, those of us in some faiths believe we have the permission to use this Earth for what we want, simply because God told us we could. Religion plays into our egos. My God is better than your god, and because of that, I will dismiss anything you say. Because if your God is not mine, than what could you possibly be when compared to me? Just as religion plays with our egos, religion is material. Not only because some of us go to church with the desire to compare clothing, but because we pay into the religion; hoping to buy an afterlife filled with riches. Nothing concerning organized religion is needed for human evolution, other than its absence.

It takes a big step for me to talk about this publicly. I risk offending many people. And although I mean no offense, I sincerely mean what I say about religion. It took me the better part of a decade to know how to put it into text. But the truth is, I've seen some of the darkest moments that religion has to offer. And because of the environment that I grew up in and then stepped out of, I can see past much of the blind faith that people express about their own religion. Circular reasoning is just that, and it doesn't do anyone any good, except for the people collecting the money trays.

Organized religion can be a very sad story for some people, especially when you take someone who was as hard working and loving as my father. I feel that my adult life was spent watching his brain turn to mush, as he neglected logic to believe what he was told as truth. I want to believe that he woke up towards the end, but me and everyone else in the House of Yahweh know that my father always did what he was told. But maybe he saw further proof of the inhumane actions towards women and children. Maybe he felt guilty that he too, denied the actions of one of their leaders convicted of child molestation. Maybe he woke up and couldn't handle the evil. Maybe he woke up and said, I can't take it anymore. I suppose this would make sense why he hung himself on someone else's property. But I will never know. I will only know that the two men that saw over my father's finances had only one concern: money.

I write these words while looking down through a clear sky toward the Mediterranean. I just left Morocco, and today is the last day of Ramadan. I just spent a month in an Arabic country, during the most religious time. I will gladly say from my first hand experience, that my preconceived notions are true. Muslims, Christians, Jews, they're more or less all the same. Just different clothes more or less. I was called a Jew in the streets of Fez by a Muslim. I've heard Christians persecute Jews and Muslims, I've heard Jews do the same. I've seen kind acts by all, but most importantly, they have all demonstrated that they would be no different with, or without their religion. I've been swindled financially by some from every group. I've been given care and kindness by some from every group as well. They are all the same people. We are all the same people. And when we think otherwise, it's because our own ego has gotten in the way.

I have to admit that being in Morocco for Ramadan was a flashback for me. Seeing the women in their burkas, seeing the prayer sessions daily, the fasting; it all reminded me of my past. And then I got to see how they treat tourists, and for the most part, I was treated like a bag of money, where if the right buttons were pushed, they would get some. I also was able to hear some religious jargon as well. "Who wrote the Koran?" I asked. "Allah wrote the Koran." "I know, but who actually wrote it?" I asked "Allah speaks through his chosen people." I don't engage in deep religious debates anymore with religious people. It's how I show them respect for what they believe. I don't care to point out the hypocrisies or illogical forms of reason. As much as I do believe and know that religion isn't a good thing, I don't need to butt into people's lives with these thoughts. What I do believe I need to do, is find compassionate ways to interact with all people. If they can see me in my own light, then maybe that can help them find their own. This book as well as my spiritual path in life is about turning poison into medicine. I wish I can say that I've done that with everything in my life that has bothered me, but I'm confident to say that I'm on that path. My father dying the way he did was life changing.

Nothing in my life has come close to such pain. But within that pain; because of the path my father, friends and mentors have guided me on, I was still able to find and practice honesty and compassion towards those who provided such great darkness. The House of Yahweh would say sometimes "Under times of most stress, do we find our true character." And if that is true, then my independence from religion still somehow allows me to be a kind and loving person who wants nothing more in this world than for every other individual to discover their own power as a human being through honesty and compassion. My father left his family. And although he did this many years ago, we watched him from a distance as some people watched me from a distance, wondering if I would ever step out. Now that my father has left this world, he cut the tie between his family and the religious organization we watched tear him apart, slowly over time.

When my father died, I felt the pain through my entire body, and I'm not afraid to know that the pain will still show up here and there, as I continue through this walk in life. A pain like this proves to me that my connection to my father transcends what I define as real. It's more real. My grief allowed me to bring in my honesty in those moments when I saw him in his casket, and when I lowered him into the ground. I can still feel the tension of the ropes as I gently lowered him down. Nothing could be more real.

A real story is a story worth sharing, and unfortunately it doesn't end just yet. I've made a particular statement that I don't think many people quite understand, and thankfully so. I believe that in many, if not most or all cases, that people die in a way that represents the way they lived. Late in the summer, over a year after my father's death I had a phone conversation with my mother. She asked me how I was doing, and I said that I'm doing well. I asked her, the same.

"I think about you everyday, mom."

"Oh that's so nice to hear you say, I think about you almost everyday." As her voice started to shift in tone.

"I feel bad about your father. I feel guilty."

"I understand that. But in the end, what happened wasn't your fault." I responded.

"Do you think you'll ever find out what happened?" She asked.

The conversation ended with her crying over the phone. I was sad that she told me she couldn't read this book, but it was the best I could do. She continued to suffer from underlying mental health issues. That was the last conversation I had with my mother. She committed suicide several months later. My brother called me in Madrid, panicking, "She did it, She did it." He cried. Sadly to say I wasn't surprised. There was a bit of a shock to hear this, but the feeling wasn't as tremendous as it was when my father died. Whether it was intentional or not, there was always a distance between my mother and I, and perhaps as a result, I was better equipped to process her passing. I hesitate to admit this, but I almost feel as if my tears were forced. It was like I cried only out of formality.

And ultimately, that everything that I have been dedicating my life to [since I had that conversation with my father that gave me closure before he died] is real. And as a friend once told me, "How else could I know I'm alive?" I do indeed believe, believe it to be true; the more we feel our emotions and are honest with them as much as we can be, the more we live, and the more we have to share with others. By no means am I happy how this book ended. But I can say that I'm very happy for me, my father and my family to be done with the House of Yahweh. It's over. For once in my life I finally feel like I can start something new.

295

ACKNOWLEDGMENTS

Writing this book has been the most liberating undertaking of my life. I tried for years to put this story down on paper, but it wasn't until being invited into the home of Michael and Peri Coleman, that the proverbial faucets turned on, and this book began to flow out freely. I had been studying Buddhism for three years prior to writing this book, as a result of listening to Herbie Hancock's Norton lectures on Jazz at Harvard University. He opened the doors to Buddhism for me, and although I do not claim to be a Buddhist, I have found most aspects of the discipline to be very helpful in processing the difficulties of my past, and those experienced after finishing the bulk of this book.

Invoking personalized principles of Buddhism is something that I began doing a few months before the faucet turned on. Speaking endlessly and writing a few hundred words everyday is something that I fully believe lead to the outpouring of the text laid before you. I hope this book becomes a beacon for any of those who have poison in their past, so that they too may know that it can be turned into medicine. And a medicine not only for themselves, but a medicine for those around them. I owe much of this process to introspection, acceptance, honesty, and compassion. All of which that can simply be boiled down to acceptance, honesty, or compassion.

The initial goal of this book was to help anyone who has escaped a cult, or escaped any situation where fundamentalism limited their freedom. There were and still are, so many beautiful and kind people in the House of Yahweh. Every day I think of their safety, and hope that this cult doesn't end in death and destruction like several other cults.

Another goal of this book was to bring my family closer together. Most people in my family had no idea what my childhood was like, and as anyone could understand, it would have been difficult for them to imagine from just a conversation or two.

It would be nearly impossible to list all the names of those who have taken part in me writing this book. So many of you have encourage me to get this out there for several years. Mike Macdonald and his dear wife Sarah Porteus helped tremendously towards the end with direction and motivation. Mike and Peri Coleman not only provided me a nest to work from, but also their shoulders to cry on many times. They have treated me like a Son, and without them, I wouldn't know what family is supposed to quite feel like. For this, I will always be forever grateful.

To all my good friends, and in particular: Thad Lawry, David Ernsberger, Simon Hughes and Obidiah Metivier, for their input, proofreads and help in life as well. I owe much of the drive for this book to all of you. Along with my close friends, I received a lot of professional help from B.G. Bradley and Joseph Candora. If it weren't for them, I don't know how long it would have taken to get this book polished and ready for distribution.

To all of the members and ex-members of the cult: I hold sincere compassion for you in my heart. I am very thankful that many of you have chosen to take control of the reigns in your life. For those of you haven't, I don't believe there is a right or wrong choice in this matter, I only hope that you can have a constant stream of joy in your life, as I have undoubtedly put myself on a path toward that direction.

Furthermore, to any of you who may be in part responsible for the deaths of those innocent lives so tragically lost, through accidents, childbirth, or so-called self-defense; May you eventually find peace in your hearts, and a way to come to terms with your actions so that you cease from living a life filled of fear for you and those close to you. My compassion goes out to you. All of you. Even you, David Heimerman, and Yisrayl Hawkins.

Finally, I dedicate my perseverance in life, my spontaneity, joy, laughter, work ethic, mischief, passion, and willingness to live; to my Mother, Ramona Lynn Ferree, and my Father, Dale Walter Salo. May you both rest in peace, and continue to visit me in my dreams until we are together, once again.

Considerations

Reviews on Amazon.com and other book review sites help significantly. Whether you have purchased this book or recieved it as a gift, I humbly ask for an honest review when the time best suits you.

Sincerely,
Brandon Salo

Made in the USA
Middletown, DE
29 April 2021